"Parents struggling with unmotivated teens, help is here! *Helping Your Unmotivated Teen* is an easy-to-read, practical guide. Melanie McNally knows where you and your teen are, and shows the path forward with warmth and understanding. Well researched and down to earth, this guide will get you and your teen back on track, with a stronger relationship as well."

—**Hunter Clarke-Fields**, author of *Raising Good Humans*, and host of the *Mindful Parenting* podcast

"Melanie McNally is a warm, clear-eyed guide for parents struggling with an unmotivated teen. Her book will help you to get back on the same team as your teenage child."

—**Tonya Lester, LCSW**, psychotherapist; *Psychology Today* blogger; and author of the upcoming book, *Pushback*

"McNally cracked the code of parenting with emotional intelligence. She broke down complex psychological concepts into playful, easy-to-digest terms. The formulas discussed in this book optimize teen (and parenting) performance, and illuminate how to make dreams attainable."

—**Stacey Willard, PsyD**, licensed clinical psychologist; and founder and executive director of Chicago Therapy and Assessment Services in Chicago, IL, and Denver, CO

"As a parent of a young child, I delved into *Helping Your Unmotivated Teen* seeking insight, and found many helpful tips to understand the complex world of adolescence. With practical advice and heartfelt anecdotes, it equips you to connect with your teens, foster their passions, and help guide them toward purpose. A must-read for parents embarking on the teenage roller coaster!"

—**Nicole Cumberbatch**, founder of The Motherhood Village, board member of Healthy Mothers Healthy Babies Coalition of Broward County, podcaster, and proud mom

"I love a good step-by-step parenting guide, and that's exactly what Melanie McNally provides in *Helping Your Unmotivated Teen*. First, she helps you understand the essentials behind motivation. Then, she walks you through each step of helping your teen create their own road map to not only define their goals, but also break them down into small steps to make them achievable. Every parent needs this guide for the teen years!"

—**Penny Williams**, parenting coach for neurodiverse families, and author of *Boy Without Instructions*

"Unlocking the potential of an unmotivated teen can feel daunting and even impossible. In this invaluable guide, Melanie McNally illuminates a path forward with research-backed insights and actionable strategies that empower both parents and teens. A beacon of hope in the often anxiety-provoking journey of raising adolescents, this book is an essential resource for any family seeking to reignite motivation and connection during these challenging years."

—**Nicole Beurkens, PhD**, licensed clinical psychologist

HELPING YOUR UNMOTIVATED TEEN

A PARENT'S GUIDE
TO UNLOCK YOUR CHILD'S POTENTIAL

MELANIE MCNALLY, PSYD

New Harbinger Publications, Inc.

Publisher's Note

NEW HARBINGER PUBLICATIONS is a registered trademark of New Harbinger Publications, Inc.

New Harbinger Publications is an employee-owned company.

Copyright © 2024 by Melanie McNally
New Harbinger Publications, Inc.
5720 Shattuck Avenue
Oakland, CA 94609
www.newharbinger.com

Cover design by Sara Christian

Acquired by Jennye Garibaldi

Edited by Jody Bower

Library of Congress Cataloging-in-Publication Data on file

Printed in the United States of America

26   25   24

10   9   8   7   6   5   4   3   2   1   First Printing

CONTENTS

INTRODUCTION

Welcome, parents and caregivers! I know how hard this part of parenting can be—the part where your adolescent knows more than you do about life, despite having been on the planet for less time. The part where your adolescent has very little interest in following your guidance and direction and would much rather learn from a random YouTuber or influencer, or even from something they overheard in the school bathroom. And I especially get how frustrating it can be to watch your adolescent waste countless hours on meaningless things while the truly important stuff piles up around them. You're here because you want the best for your teen. You want them to have passion and a sense of purpose. You want them to plan and stay on top of responsibilities without constantly nagging them to do so. And you want them to have some direction in life, to have things that they're actively working toward. Well, you have come to the right place.

While I'm not a parent myself, I've worked specifically with adolescents since 2013 as a clinical psychologist and brain coach. I've seen my share of teens who appear lazy but who are just lacking structure and routine. I've worked with countless adolescents who procrastinate on every little detail of their life, but once given a good system that's unique to them and their lifestyle, get things done. I've worked alongside teens who appear to wander aimlessly from interest to interest, picking up a new one with excitement and then dropping it once it gets hard or boring—until they find something that gives them purpose, and then they're unstoppable.

Sometimes my role is as easy as helping them find a passion or creating a clear road map to get them going. Other times, it's teaching them how to use a planner or giving them an understanding of how their brain works. But no matter which element we focus on, it always starts with listening. Listening to what they think is important, what they feel most strongly about, and where they think their challenges lie. I've learned that listening is the most valuable skill I have. Yes, sometimes teens are more open with someone on the outside than a parent, but I also know that when parents can't or won't listen to their teen, things get ugly pretty quickly. Conversations elevate to arguments or, even worse, to silence. When a teen thinks their parent doesn't listen, they're likely to shut down and stop sharing altogether. As we go through this book together, I hope you'll keep this idea in mind. When you're talking with your teen about this book, practice your listening skills. Hold back judgment and criticism and get good at asking, "Do you want me to listen, or do you need help with problem solving right now?"

I don't want to sugarcoat things. Helping your teen won't always be easy and smooth—for the teen or for you. There will be bumps and detours along the way. There will be times that you feel like things are moving at a snail's pace when all you want to do is speed up the process. There will be frustration and disappointment. Challenges will arise, new problems will replace old ones, and there might even be some cursing and yelling. But I wrote this book to be a guide for you, giving you information that will help you understand the *why* behind what you're doing, providing you with tools that are easy to implement immediately, and teaching you how to help your teen, no matter where they are in their own life.

Motivation

When you think of motivation, what comes to mind? Take a moment to reflect on the following questions:

★   How do you view motivation?

★   What do you think motivates humans?

★   How do you motivate yourself to do hard things?

★   How do you motivate your teen to do hard things?

Many people have a strictly behavioral perspective on motivation; they think we're motivated to do things that reward us and we're less likely to do things that are punitive. But if it were that simple, teens would strive for high grades at school and would avoid doing things that they know would get them in trouble. They would always do their chores at home if there was an allowance attached, and wouldn't steal their sibling's clothes if it meant risking the loss of a privilege. The behavioral perspective includes self-determination theory, which states that other things motivate us as well, like autonomy, competence, and relatedness (Deci and Ryan 1985). In contrast, when there is excessive control, lack of challenge, or a lack of connection, motivation is significantly disrupted (Ryan and Deci 2000).

If your teen isn't allowed to choose their project topic and instead has to do an assigned topic, they likely groan before even opening the laptop to research it. Or if the orchestra teacher has them playing the same songs repeatedly, ones you've heard your teen master long ago, it's likely a struggle to get them to practice anymore. Perhaps you've noticed that your teen is less likely to practice their swing alone at the batting cages than when they get hitting practice with their team. You've seen the effect of autonomy, competence, and relatedness first-hand on your teen's motivation.

Sophia tried out for the high school track team this year, mostly because that's what all her friends were doing. She surprised herself when not only did she make the team, but she also turned out to be a good sprinter. Her parents were thrilled, because in the past Sophia usually fought them on playing organized sports. They ended up either bribing her or arguing with her to get her to show up for anything they signed her up for, whether it was dance, softball, or swim. So they were surprised to find that Sophia loved going to track practice with her friends and made even more friends on the team. Meets were especially fun for her because she was able to spend an entire day with her friends, and they would usually go out to eat or to someone's house afterward.

Sophia's coach worked with her to improve her running style and by midseason, she was winning races against older and more experienced sprinters. She begged her parents to purchase expensive running shoes like those worn by her closest friends on the team. Her parents surprised her with a pair after her last meet, where she placed in the top ten on all her events. At the next practice, she and her friends took a picture showcasing their matching shoes, immediately posted it, and received a ton of likes and comments. Sophia thought to herself, "I love track."

Psychologists define motivation as "the impetus that gives purpose or direction to behavior and operates in humans at a conscious or unconscious level" (APA Dictionary). Typically, motivation is broken down into intrinsic (internal) motivators and extrinsic (external) motivators. For Sophia, her intrinsic motivators are the fun she has at track practice and the sense of belonging she gains from her friends there. Her extrinsic motivators are the positive feedback she receives from others when she performs well and the new shoes her parents purchased for her. While we each have unique things that provide us with intrinsic and extrinsic motivation, they all share the same foundation. Most people are intrinsically motivated by things they enjoy, are curious about, or find fun, while most people are extrinsically motivated by promotions, grades, rewards, or bonuses.

Many parents tend to view motivation solely through an extrinsic lens of reward and punishment. Give a privilege or special treat to get the behavior you want, take away a privilege or right when you see behavior you don't want. While this type of motivational system can be highly effective at times, most parents don't want to rely on it as the only mechanism for motivation. They want to see their teen motivated intrinsically, by their own passions, interests, and excitement.

Think of the last time you saw your teen genuinely excited about something—so excited that they required no reminders or push to do it. What were they doing? Don't worry that your teen is only excited about screens, relationships, or shopping; we'll sort that out in a bit. The point is, if your teen has something that they're so excited about, no matter what it is, that they require little push from you to do it, they have intrinsic motivation. I'll show you how to find connections and overlaps so that their intrinsic motivators will help them in other areas of life, even those areas where you must nag, push, or bribe to bring them to life.

Extrinsic motivators might lead your teen to the water, but intrinsic motivators will get them to swim. For example, your teen might pay only enough attention in physics class to keep from getting in trouble and get a decent grade, but until they're intrinsically motivated, they're unlikely to do much more. But maybe one day they get an assignment where they have to watch an action movie and dissect the fight scenes to prove how the actor's movements are or aren't possible—suddenly, your teen is curious about physics. They annoy everyone in the house as they prove how characters in video games don't make sense or how the scenes in your favorite show couldn't possibly happen. They're talking about physics because they're interested, not because of a grade or test.

Intrinsic motivators will keep your teen on track long after their friends lose interest in the same activity. They will help your teen stay focused, even on the days they feel apathetic or lost. You don't have to fight with your teen to do the things that intrinsically motivate them—you might even find that you have to fight with them to stop! In other words, your teen is intrinsically motivated when they do what interests them purely for the enjoyment of the activity (Hektner and Csíkszentmihályi 1996). There's no external reward attached—or if there is, they're not concerned with getting it.

The Components of Motivation

Steven Kotler is a writer and journalist who has dedicated his career to understanding and teaching people how to achieve peak performance. In his book *The Art of Impossible*, he contends that motivation encompasses three skillsets: drive, grit, and goals (Kotler 2021). We're going to focus on each skillset in this book. Each section starts with an overview to give you the lay of the land, followed by a deep dive so you get a good understanding of the research behind each component, and then a chapter on action steps so you have tools to start using immediately.

In brief, drive is made up of curiosity, passion, autonomy, mastery, and purpose (Pink 2009; Kotler 2021). Grit is our passion and perseverance for long-term goals (Duckworth 2016). Goals provide the road map for us to follow. When we integrate each of these elements into our behavior, we're motivated to move forward.

Let's look at how each might appear in a highly motivated teen:

Sydney is determined to make the college dive team at her dream school (purpose). She's loved the sport for as long as she can remember (passion) and is extremely skilled at it (mastery). She competes at the state level and works with a diving coach five days a week. There are days when she doesn't want to get out of bed for her 5:30 a.m. practices, but she rarely misses one (grit). She and her coach have a solid plan in place, which she believes will help her make the college team. She's chosen the dives she's most excited about to learn (autonomy) and set milestones for learning each one (goal setting).

Sydney's story demonstrates how the components of drive—curiosity, passion, purpose, autonomy, and mastery—push her to work hard. Her grit gives her the ability to stick with things, even when she must get out of bed early and practice the monotony of small moves again and again. And her breakdown of goals, from the major one of getting on the college team down to breaking a complex dive up into small moves, gives her the practical day-to-day steps she needs to stay focused.

Imagine if one of these components were missing. What would be different if Sydney didn't have passion? She'd likely stay up late doing things she finds more interesting and arrive to early morning practice fatigued. Or what if Sydney didn't have grit? How would she stick with the monotony of practicing backflips repeatedly on dry land and then into a foam pit? How would she make it to those early morning practices so consistently? And imagine if she didn't have clear goals to focus on. What if she didn't have the overall purpose of getting onto the college dive team or the goals of perfecting specific moves? She might lose focus or arrive to practice without a plan and become easily distracted by anything that crosses her path.

Drive, grit, and goals are the key ingredients to motivating your teen. Once you're done with this book, you'll feel ready to help your teen no matter which area they're struggling in.

Motivation and Teens

It's no secret that adolescence is a tough period, for the teen and for the parent (Casey, Duhoux, and Cohen 2010). Teens crave more independence, while parents pour on more responsibility. Teens want to explore new challenges and activities, while parents worry about them facing demanding environments and situations. Teens push for more control over their decisions, and parents push back with harsher consequences for poor ones. It doesn't matter if you've parented other teens before; the one in front of you now brings their own unique personality and generational input to the picture. It can feel like a never-ending game of struggle and balance. Parents and teens each get frustrated and wonder when things will improve.

Most of us find it hard to resist short-term gratification in order to reach long-term goals (Casey, Duhoux, and Cohen 2010). Teens are even more likely to do what feels good in the moment, even if it has the potential to detract from something they want in the future. Sydney was able to resist temptations so she could focus on diving; however, many teens do not share her level of commitment.

Interestingly, research shows that teens are more motivated by rewards and incentives than are adults (Cauffman et al. 2010). In fact, when teens are between 13 and 17 years old, their response to rewards peaks (Steinberg et al. 2009). What does this mean for you? Trying to pay your spouse to empty the dishwasher each night likely isn't going to work, but paying your teen to do it might. It's totally fine to attach incentives to desired behaviors to motivate your teen! Because their brains respond to rewards in a way that adults' brains don't, some sort of incentive might just be the push they need to develop drive, grit, or goals. While you wouldn't want incentives to be the only mechanism you use to motivate your teen, it's okay to do it from time to time, especially when they need a jump-start. Maybe you reward your low-energy teen for spending time exploring new things that pique their interest—what I like to call "curiosities"—to get them out of their room on the weekends. Or maybe you allow your teen with the huge goal to have friends sleep over after they've tackled the first of many steps that will lead to their desired result.

Additionally, teens are more motivated by peer influence than they are by adult influence—especially when it comes to risky decisions (Gardner and Steinberg 2005). For example, researchers found that teens make riskier driving choices when in the presence of a peer as opposed to when alone (Gardner and Steinberg 2005). While this propensity toward riskier decisions decreases in young adulthood, it can motivate teens who need a little more of a kick in the rump. Perhaps the shy teen who's afraid to go outside their comfort zone might be more motivated to try something new when with a team or their friends. In contrast, the teen who constantly makes risky choices might benefit from doing some things solo, especially if the other activities are full of temptations.

Sometimes parents think their teen lacks motivation, but they aren't seeing the whole picture.

Jason is a sophomore in high school and his parents believe he hasn't really found his "thing" yet. He does the bare minimum for his homework—instead, he plays music with friends, goes to concerts on the weekends, and constantly listens to music. He spends his free time watching music videos and playing his drums, and he recently started a band with some friends, which takes up even more time with practicing and trying to book gigs. His parents are frustrated that he doesn't help out more at home or have any school-related extracurriculars. They've tried to "bribe" him and paid him to attend school clubs, gave him an allowance, and threatened him with the loss of his phone. While these things help in the short term, nothing seems to stick long-term. They want to see him have more of a direction in life, show effort, and work hard.

On the surface, Jason appears to be lacking in all the areas of motivation—drive, grit, and goals. But let's look a bit closer. Jason spends most of his free time at home listening to music, watching music videos, and playing his drums. He goes to concerts on the weekends. He and his friends recently started a band and now try to go out and get gigs. He's driven by music! He's so curious and passionate about music that he spends all his free time doing it. He's constantly practicing, creating, and watching videos to learn more, and he even started a business around it with his band. He's showing grit, as practicing an instrument can be a monotonous task. He might be lacking in clear goals and could benefit from having more direction. His parents would probably also like to see some of this motivation translate over to schoolwork and household chores, but as far as having some of the components of motivation in place, he's off to a pretty good start.

Like many teens, Jason has found something he's interested in that doesn't quite align with what his parents want for him. It seems like his parents would prefer to see his motivation be used on things other than music. In such cases, parents can miss out on opportunity. Jason has drive and grit; these are transferrable. When a teen has drive and grit in one area, they can transfer these skills to other things. Jason sticks with the monotony and the difficulty of practicing, creating, testing things out, failing, sitting still for long periods, and being laser-focused. These skills that he possesses can apply to other areas of life like physics, cleaning the bathroom, college applications, or student leadership positions. It's just a matter of helping him make the connections.

Motivation is the force behind most of what we do. Even as adults, if we're not motivated by purpose or pay, many of us might not show up to work each day. If we're not able to stick with things when they're challenging, we might not fully train the family dog and end up with a pet who jumps on the countertops and eats the garbage. And if we lack clear goals, we might find ourselves easily distracted and realize that we didn't accomplish much at the end of the day.

Major Obstacles to Motivation in Teens

Adults need motivation to get things done. Teens do too—but they have many more challenges facing them.

For one thing, teens' brains aren't yet fully developed; they don't have the necessary neural networks in place that allow for some of the key parts that make motivation possible. Goal-creating is a complex task. It requires planning, organizing, and prioritization, all of which occur in the prefrontal cortex. And guess which part of the brain is the last to develop? Teens face another big challenge when it comes to motivation: managing distractions. Being able to manage distractions allows them to focus on their passions and stick with things when they get boring.

Let's address the elephant in the room now...

Is Your Teen Addicted to Screens?

A complaint I hear from many parents goes something like this: *My teen just stares at their screen all day. They use it for school, get distracted constantly while doing their schoolwork, take forever to get their work done, and then scroll mindlessly or watch ridiculous videos until bedtime. How am I supposed to get them motivated when I can't get them off their screen?*

Devices are designed to be addictive. It doesn't matter if we're watching videos, mindlessly scrolling, or gaming; there is major sensory overload happening. And that sensory overload is extremely enticing. Our brains want more—more action, more stimulation, more spots in our brain to light up. The real world just can't compete. Learning, reading, even talking are less stimulating. So what do we do to combat this real-world boredom? We have multiple tabs open while the teacher is talking, go back and forth between a video and a book while reading, and check our phone while our friend is telling a story.

And that's not even including what happens when we receive notifications, whether it's a text alert, a DM, or the red bubble showing how many unread emails we have waiting for us. We feel stress when a notification pops up; when we feel stress, cortisol (the "fight-or-flight" hormone) is released. We feel relief and pleasure when we check the notification and dopamine (the "feel-good" hormone) is dumped—and then we want more of that. Plus, our attention is diverted, so it will take time and effort to get back on track. Research shows that it takes twenty-three minutes for our brains to get back to where they were before reading the notification or alert (Glaveski 2019). Even if you didn't click on the notification, it still grabbed your attention, and information had to be processed. Your brain lost where it was and must reset to get back on track. If you did click on it, you're now likely to read the message, respond (or at least think of a response), and perhaps even check other alerts that are waiting. You're likely going to lose much more than the twenty-three minutes; you might even lose your motivation.

How much time do you spend on devices? How do you handle notifications and alerts? Do you look every time your phone buzzes or dings? Where does your phone charge at night—in another room, far from the bed, or on the nightstand next to your pillow? Do you check your phone or device first thing in the morning and the last thing before going to sleep? Are you able to wait in line, or even at a red light, without checking your phone?

Managing attention is hard enough for an adult to do, despite our fully developed brains and without having grown up with smartphones. I once timed myself to see how long I could go without checking my phone while writing, thinking I was going to impress myself. I lasted seven minutes and forty-three seconds. Not even eight minutes. And I knew I was timing myself. So trust me, no judgment here.

I'm not asking these questions to make anyone feel bad. I'm asking you to reflect on your own behaviors *before* making your teen change theirs. While I hear parents complain about their teens' screen use, I also hear teens' frustration with their parents' "do as I say, not as I do" approach to the topic. If you're planning on making some changes at home, I suggest starting from the top down. Make changes first as parents and then implement them as family rules.

How might you do this? One suggestion is to buy alarm clocks (remember those? Yes, they still exist.) and put one in your bedroom, leaving the phones to charge in the kitchen every night. Leave your phone on silent and in a drawer when hanging out with the family and be conscious about checking it, rather than letting your phone decide when you should look at it.

Once these new behaviors are a habit, buy alarm clocks for each bedroom and make all phones go into the kitchen at night. Require that phones/devices are put away during family or dinner time. Because your teen has already observed you doing these very same things, it won't feel like a punishment. As you start to change your behavior first and then implement family rules second, you'll notice positive results that will motivate you to keep going. You might even notice that, because people aren't sitting around staring at their devices, there's time to take the dog on a walk, prepare for the next day, or even read (gasp!) a book.

Is Your Teen Depressed?

Sometimes a parent might find that their teen isn't curious or passionate about anything. They show minimal interest in relationships and they can't find any activity that lights them up. Sometimes parents notice that their teen doesn't seem to have any energy to stick with hard things and gets overwhelmed when talking about a direction forward. Perhaps their teen doesn't want to engage in life most days; no matter how hard the parent pushes, rewards, or offers incentives, their teen just isn't interested. This can be a scary place for a parent (and a teen) to live. And it might be more than a lack of motivation; it might be that this teen is experiencing depression or another mental health issue.

Teens experiencing depression lack motivation for most things that life requires of them. They usually struggle at school, home, and with friendships. They don't do homework or chores; they don't hang out with anyone. They might appear irritable most of the time and complain of fatigue. They might no longer want to do things they previously enjoyed. You might notice that they're just not performing at the level they were before. They might be withdrawing into their rooms, screens, and themselves, not wanting to share with you what's truly going on. Or if they do share, they tell you they feel like a burden or that it would be easier for everyone if they weren't around anymore.

If you notice that your teen's lack of motivation is more than not being able to manage distractions, more than not having found a purpose or passion, and more than not being able to stick with things when they get hard or boring, consider talking to a mental health professional. You can reach out to the school psychologist or counselor, pediatrician, or a local therapist. They'll ask some questions, meet with you and your teen, and help you determine if the lack of motivation is due to depression or something else.

How to Use This Book

I want this book to be a helpful guide, like having a friend in your corner who's there to give support when you need it, advice when you're ready for it, tools when you're begging for them, and reminders that you're doing your absolute best. How do I know you're doing your best? Because I work with parents just like you—parents who have loving intentions, are willing to learn and change, and are rooting for their adolescent so fiercely that they sometimes neglect their own needs. I hope you know this about yourself too. I hope that you're able to cut yourself some slack when you screw up (because you will) and that you find humor when your teen calls you out (because they will).

This book is set up to give you information and tools. The information is here so you understand the *why* behind the things your teen does and the purpose behind the tools. Understanding this will help with your own motivation when things get tough. You don't need to memorize anything; you can refer back to things as often as you need. You might find that some information applies to where your teen is now in their life, but later you need other parts of the book. Take what you need as you go and leave the rest for when you're ready.

I sometimes ask you to assess yourself in certain areas and to create changes in your own life. This isn't because you're failing as a parent (hard no on that one!) or a total screwup as an adult (definitely not!). It's because we *all* benefit from growth and positive change, no matter where in our lives we currently are. I'll ask you to look at yourself and your behaviors to facilitate your own growth, but also because I want your teen to see you creating changes. There's something extremely powerful about making changes together. Not only will it put you and your teen on even ground, in that you're both doing something hard, but it also normalizes the process. If you and your teen are both eliminating distractions, for example, you're modeling effort and determination while also demonstrating that it's perfectly normal to struggle with distractions. You're showing that you're willing to take action to deal with such struggles. When parents do things in secrecy and behind closed doors, the adolescents in their lives miss out on seeing that positive change takes work and occurs throughout life, not just during the teen years.

Everything I write is based on the research that I use in my work with adolescents. I provide citations and a reference list in case you want to go deeper into what I share. I'm so excited for you as you move forward on this journey. I know that we're going to get your teen more motivated! I can't wait to hear from you about how your adolescent found their passions, discovered their purpose, became grittier, and reached their goals. I know they're going to accomplish great things and make this world a better place.

CHAPTER 1

WHAT IS DRIVE?

DRIVE IS OUR INTERNAL COMPASS. In *Drive: The Surprising Truth About What Motivates Us*, author Daniel Pink builds upon self-determination theory, which says autonomy, competence, and relatedness are the main motivational drivers, by adding the need for purpose (2009). Purpose is the underlying reason *why* behind our behavior. Flow researcher Steven Kotler adds curiosity and passion (2021). For both adults or teens, if we're not curious about something or if we lack passion for it, we're not going to be driven to stick with it.

So the key components for drive are curiosity, passion, purpose, autonomy, and mastery. We'll do a deep dive into each area in the next chapter but for now, let's consider them from a more general perspective. As you read through the first three areas below, notice how they build upon one another: curiosity leads to passion, which creates purpose.

Curiosity

When we're genuinely curious about something, we want to learn more about it. The American Psychological Association defines curiosity as "the impulse or desire to investigate, observe, or gather information, particularly when the material is novel or interesting." It's not something we have much control over and can occur spontaneously. It's not a conscious choice that we make; we don't think, "I'm going to be curious about working on cars today." As we're each unique, what's novel and interesting to one person might not be to another.

Think about a young child who's curious about dinosaurs. You don't have to push dinosaur books or figurines onto them; they're reaching for those items every time they see one. They want to learn as much as they can about every type of dinosaur that ever existed. They draw pictures of them for fun, watch videos about them whenever allowed, and ask for dinosaur-themed toys as gifts. Curiosity in young children is usually easy to see; they're almost too curious sometimes! They explore their world constantly, which sometimes leads to being distracted, asking incessant questions, or trying something dangerous.

Consider what this means for your teen. Curiosity is an impulse or desire that can appear spontaneously when the material is novel or interesting. When we flip that around, we see that curiosity is not something that we can schedule or force with just any subject or topic. But how often do parents and educators attempt to do just that? How often have you tried to get your teen curious about something that you thought they should be interested in, whether it was because you liked that thing when you were their age or because their friends are into it? But as you can see from the very definition of curiosity, that's not how it works.

Maybe your teen is curious about computer programming and talks with their friends about the flaws in the newest trendy game, critiquing the movements of the characters and how the action sequences could be designed better. You notice them trying different moves in the game to see if it improves the flow. You're not pushing this onto your teen; it's a natural curiosity that's emerging right in front of you. It's material that they find interesting and it's happening on their time. They're following a desire. If given space to explore this curiosity, they might start dabbling in designing their own video game, sign up for electives that are focused on computer programming, and save up money to buy the necessary software and equipment. And all of this happened simply because you gave your teen the space to explore.

Passion

If we're passionate about what we're doing, we want to keep going. Passion can be an intense feeling or conviction. In its strongest form, passion is overwhelming and unavoidable. But there's a less powerful version of passion, which is more of a strong enthusiasm or devotion toward something. So even if we're not overwhelmed or feeling an intense conviction for something, we can be extremely enthusiastic about it.

I love spotting passions in people, especially the adolescents I know or with whom I work. I knew a teen who was intensely passionate about music; she wrote and sang her own songs, created soundtracks for background, recorded her own music videos, performed at school concerts, and studied other musicians to learn from their methods. It was passion to the core. But I don't often see passion in adolescents today. Most of them are coming to me because they're lacking it and need help finding some. The reason? There's less time and space to explore curiosities. If a teen doesn't have a schedule that allows them to follow an impulse to investigate things that are new or interesting—to get curious—how can they develop enthusiasm or an intense conviction about anything? The musical teen above took lots of different music classes as a child; while she dropped some of them, she found that she loved guitar. Without much parental input, she was able to explore her musical curiosities until she found her passion.

It can be hard for some parents when their teen has passion for something that pulls them away from what the parent thinks they should be doing. Imagine a teen who's fiercely passionate about science fiction novels and movies, but has parents who want them playing sports and on a team. What if these parents ignore how this teen has started writing their own stories, and instead of putting them in creative writing or theater camps for the summer, signs them up for basketball camp? As discussed in the introduction, it's important that parents be open to the idea that your teen's passions may not match the vision you have for them. Even if they have enthusiasm for things you have zero interest in, or feel intensely about issues you think are ridiculous, keep in mind that we want teens to have passions. We want them to feel intensely, to have strong convictions, and to be enthusiastic. It's good for their mental wellness too (which I discuss in the next chapter).

Perhaps your teen is passionate about fashion. No matter what the situation, they *must* put together the perfect outfit. They're always watching fashion videos and contests, talking your ear off about trends, and begging you to subscribe to fashion blogs for them. Maybe you've noticed that your teen loves thrift stores and has started to sew their own creations from vintage clothing. They spend hours sewing, watching videos from designers, or walking through their favorite clothing store. No one's bribing, coercing, or rewarding them for any of this. Their passion is pushing them forward. Even if you're not into fashion yourself or view it as a total waste of time and resources, this is what's motivating them. They have something that they enjoy—maybe something that's leading them somewhere even bigger, to as sense of their purpose in life.

Purpose

When there's a purpose behind our behavior, we want to see it through. Purpose gives meaning to our actions and lives. It's the *why* behind what we do. It can be huge, grand, even a bit abstract, like solving the youth mental health crisis or always acting from a place of kindness. But purpose also can be a mental goal or aim that directs us and keeps us moving forward. This form of purpose might be a bit more specific, like writing books that help youth or doing yoga to learn inner peace. Yet so many of us have no idea what our *why* is behind most of our actions. So many people are moving through life without understanding their reasons for doing things or a clear goal. And when we don't have a reason or goal, it's easy to get distracted and end up filling our days with things that don't really add up to much. When teens have purpose, their days have direction, and they tend to be more focused overall. And purpose in one area of life affects all areas of life.

As you consider what we've covered so far, do you see the thread? Curiosity leads to passion, and passion leads to purpose. Let's look at this a bit more closely. A child who is curious about art might take art classes. They might explore different media by taking painting, drawing, collage, and pottery classes. This child turns into a teen who loves pottery and spends more time on this one medium, letting the others fizzle out. Your house is overflowing with mugs, vases, and bowls, and everyone in the family knows what to expect as a gift from your teen when it comes to the holidays. They become determined to attend art school and find ways to make their college application extra attractive—working at a pottery store, interning with a local artist, taking every art elective their high school offers. They have a mental aim that is directing their actions every day. They have a reason to get out of bed in the morning, do their homework, and stay on top of their responsibilities.

Purpose in one area of life is contagious. When your teen has a purpose, it bleeds over into other areas. The artist is focused primarily on creating art and getting into art school, but her ability to focus is going to help her in all areas of life. Because of her purpose, she's less likely to waste her time on things that aren't as important, like scrolling mindlessly or drinking alcohol (even if her peers are doing it). Because she has mental aim, she's more likely to take care of other responsibilities, like getting homework done so she has the grades to take those electives she desires or the time to intern. Having purpose is so good for teens. Even if you're not entirely in agreement with their purpose, even if you view art school as a waste of money and can't imagine how your teen will ever be able to support themselves as an artist, it's a good thing. If you're not sold on it yet, just imagine the opposite. Imagine your teen not having any direction or aim at all, not having a reason to exist, and not having anything to persist at. No one wants that for their teen, especially you.

Autonomy

When we have autonomy, we have control. In self-determination theory, autonomy is defined as the experience of acting from choice, rather than pressure. Think of the jobs you've had; can you recall one where your supervisor gave you no choice in how to do your work? Perhaps you were micromanaged constantly and told how to talk to customers, what to wear, or what to write in your emails. Maybe you were pressured to select certain projects to work on and weren't allowed to focus on what you truly wanted to do. It didn't feel good, did it? When we're put in situations where we have very little choice or are under pressure to act specific ways, we might get the job done; but we're not very likely to get much out of it or to want to stick with it for long.

Parenting research supports the importance of autonomy. Parents with an *authoritarian* style set strict rules and punishments and allow very little choice for their teens. They're the parents who tell their teens how to dress, what electives to take, who to be friends with, and what clubs or activities to sign up for. In contrast, parents with an *authoritative* style problem solve and collaborate with their teens and allow natural consequences to occur. This type of parent sets expectations and parameters for behavior, but then allows the teen to choose their actions within them. If the teen makes a mistake or if it doesn't work out, the parent might help find solutions; however, they're not constantly running in to rescue or fix. Then there are *permissive* and *neglectful* parenting styles where the parent either rarely enforces rules or provides guidance, or is uninvolved and absent. Research shows that parents with an authoritative style tend to raise teens who are resilient and well-adjusted (Dewar 2023). When teens have autonomy, they learn how to be self-reliant, make healthier choices, and have fewer emotional and behavioral problems.

When it comes to your teen, it's not about handing over the car keys and letting them use the car whenever they want. It's about letting them know the rules around using the family car (have to check with others first, fill up the tank when done, etc.) and when they're allowed to use it (chores and homework need to be done, have to have a certain grade point average, etc.), and then allowing them to figure things out within those guidelines. If they make a mistake or bad choice, the natural consequence is losing driving privileges for a set amount of time. If they handle the responsibility well, they get to keep using the family car. You're giving them some control and allowing them to make healthy choices (or not). This is autonomy in action.

You've likely observed what happens when your teen gets to decide which electives to take or what activities to sign up for. If someone else makes those choices for them, they're much less likely to feel motivated. Think of a time when your teen had very little control over their actions. For example, perhaps you told them which jobs they could apply for. Your teen may have shown up physically for work, but mentally, they weren't present or engaged. Or maybe you created new family rules at home without any input from your teen, only to find that your teen didn't care at all about these carefully crafted guidelines and ignored them. When you bring autonomy into the equation, your teen is much more likely to be motivated.

Mastery

Mastery helps with motivation by giving us the skillset we need to do the activity or task. If we don't have the skills to do something, we'll feel overwhelmed and give up. Even if it's something we'd like to accomplish, we're going to need a lot of extra pushes to make it over the hump. Think of a time when you were learning a new skill and how difficult it was to keep moving forward initially; however, once you became skilled, it was much easier to progress. Maybe you needed to become proficient at lifting weights when you started doing CrossFit, and until you were, you had to bribe and coerce yourself to make it to classes each week. Once you started to get the hang of things though, your motivation to attend shot up.

Mastering skills takes much more cognitive effort when it comes to teens. That's because the adolescent phase comes with an *imaginary audience*, meaning that adolescents see themselves as objects of others' attention and evaluation (Elkind and Bowen 1979). Perhaps your teen has shared that they think everyone is always watching them at school or judging their every move, causing them to feel anxious when walking down the school hallway or speaking in front of the class. Maybe their imaginary audience causes them to skip auditions for the school play, despite their desire to be an actor, or to not sign up for the talent show even though it's all they've been talking about for weeks. This phase is unique to the adolescent years and won't last forever. However, it can be the very thing that holds them back from working on mastery.

When a teen is learning a new skill, they're focused on improvement and progress. Maybe your teen is working to learn a kickflip on their skateboard, watching videos of pro skaters repeatedly and then practicing in the driveway alone. As soon as they land one successfully, they decide to try out their new moves at the local skate park. They see older kids there, ones who have been doing kickflips for much longer, and immediately feel anxious. As they warm up, they become insecure and think that everyone is judging them, laughing at their beginner-level skills. Instead of trying out their new trick, they stick with what they know how to do well and don't challenge themselves. The imaginary audience prevents them from practicing their trick and perhaps even getting valuable feedback from those who have been doing it much longer. Their path to mastery stalls.

Before we move on to a deeper understanding of drive, here's an exercise to help you assess your own drive as well as that of your teen.

ASSESSING DRIVE

Drive is such an important part of motivation that there are entire books written on the topic. Let's take a moment to assess drive—both yours and your teen's. Grab a piece of paper or a journal and something to write with (and maybe a drink of water, as you will want to take your time on this) and answer the following questions:

- List out ten things you're curious about. Be as specific as you can. For example, don't just write "wildlife;" write "signs and tracks of animals in a coniferous forest." Take your time and really think about this before moving on.

- Write down your top five passions. Again, get specific. Instead of "music," you might write "playing drums in a punk band."

- Identify your purpose and write it down. What's your guiding principle or life mission statement? What kind of legacy do you want to leave? Take a few minutes to think about it, then write it out in 1–3 sentences.

- Where in your life do you feel you have the most control over your decisions? List out the places and the specific areas within each. For instance, you might write "Home: how to organize it, where most items are kept, the vibe, the design, what we eat, food in the kitchen, what time I get up, what time I go to bed, how I spend my free time, when and how I interact with others..."

- Where in your life do you feel mastery? Where do you have the skillset to complete the necessary tasks and to continue to progress? Again, get specific. Perhaps it's a particular project at work, a task you do at home, or a social or recreational activity you do for fun.

Once you've answered these questions for yourself, get a new piece of paper. This time, answer the above questions for your teen. List out what they appear to be curious and passionate about, what you think their purpose is, where you think they feel most in control, and where they experience mastery. If your teen is willing, you can give them the questions and have them answer for themselves. You can compare what you wrote for them and what they wrote for themselves to see how accurate you were and to gain a better understanding of your teen.

Use this assessment to see which areas of drive your teen is strong in and which areas are weaker. Keep their strengths and weaknesses in mind as you read through the following chapters.

CHAPTER 2

A DEEPER DIVE INTO DRIVE

Max went off to college with an undeclared major and no idea of what he wanted to do with his life. His first year was spent taking general education requirements, meeting people, and adjusting to college life. He often skipped classes and spent the weekend partying with people he barely knew. He felt anxious, lost, and lonely much of the time. As his second semester was ending, one of his favorite professors mentioned that he needed someone to help with a research project he was running. Max learned more about the project, and since he really didn't want to return home for the summer, he took the job. In time, he became interested—not in the actual content but about how research projects are created. He asked questions about funding and learned about grants. He asked about getting approval and the rights of volunteers and learned about boards and policies. He met other researchers who were working on other projects, completely different from his own, but just as useful and important. He became friends with some of the other students working on the various projects and played Frisbee golf with them on the weekends.

When it was time to resume classes in the fall, he decided to switch out an elective so he could take a class on grantwriting. He found he enjoyed his classes now and wanted to do well, which created better sleep habits. He also was more engaged in classes, which created more meaningful relationships with his peers and professors. He continued to work with the professor on other research projects over every break he had. That work led to classes the following semester on research methods, social psychology, and public policy. He was becoming more focused at school, which boosted his self-confidence. He started listening to inspiring podcasts and exercising. By the end of his second year, he declared his major in public policy, knowing that he wanted to focus on designing research projects that will create meaningful change in the lives of underserved populations. He felt motivated and excited now that he had a direction in life.

Let's take a deeper dive into the different components of drive.

Curiosity Creates More Curiosity

Max's story shows how a simple curiosity can lead to passion and purpose. His interest in research design developed into a passion, which resulted in a purpose of creating impactful studies. There were likely lots of other things Max became curious about along the way; he may have followed other pathways simultaneously. Some of these may have fizzled out quickly while others continued developing. As Max's story demonstrates, his initial goal was to find something that would allow him to stay on campus for the summer! It wasn't the noble pursuit of knowledge or a desire to find meaning in life; it was simply, "I wonder how I could afford to live here, rather than have to return home for summer break." As George Loewenstein put it, "Curiosity is superficial in the sense that it can arise, change focus, or end abruptly" (1994). But as we can see, for Max, no matter how superficial the initial curiosity, passion and purpose were just around the corner.

Curiosity is the desire to acquire new information and is often accompanied by positive emotions like contentment or joy. But as Loewenstein points out, it can shift and change quickly. Often, parents become frustrated with the ease that teens shift interests. They'll say things like, "My teen never sticks with anything," or "I just wish they could control their impulses better." But that's not how curiosity works. Its very nature produces impulsive behavior! It's different with purpose. When your teen is exploring new interests, they might not stick with things very long; however, when curiosity has become a sense of purpose, you want them to develop grit so they can stay with it for the long haul. (We'll cover grit in the next section.)

Interestingly, adolescents show better memory for information that they're genuinely curious about (Gruber and Fandakova 2021). If your teen is intrigued by what they're learning in biology class, they'll likely be able to recall that information more easily. If you notice that your teen tends to recall what they did in one class more than another, if they perform better on tests in one class, or if they go above and beyond on a project, you might be witnessing curiosity in action.

The imaginary audience (discussed in chapter 1) can make curiosity particularly tricky for a teen to navigate. While they might want to ask a ton of questions in class, fear of being evaluated and judged by their peers might dampen any show of excitement. It's important that your teen has space to explore their interests outside of school and away from their imaginary audience. Attending camps or after-school programs in different districts or taking virtual classes could give them the space they need.

Mindset also plays an important role in the development of curiosities. A *fixed mindset* is at work when we view traits like intelligence, abilities, or talents as inherently stable, whereas a *growth mindset* allows us to view these same traits as learnable and capable of growth and improvement. Mindset affects self-perception by creating a belief in whether or not we're able to do something; researchers have found that it also impacts the development of curiosities and interests in young adults (O'Keefe, Dweck, and Walton 2018). When college students viewed interests with a fixed mindset, they were less likely to explore new interests and more likely to give up when things get difficult. The more fixed a student's mindset was, the more they expected to have endless motivation to pursue an interest. In contrast, students with a growth mindset were more likely to keep pursuing curiosities even when things became difficult (O'Keefe, Dweck, and Walton 2018).

Passion Develops Out of Curiosity

Passion goes beyond curiosity in that it involves a personal identification with the area of interest, more positive emotions, more commitment, and higher likelihood of persistence (Chen et al. 2021). Mindset also plays a role in the development of passions (Chen et al. 2021). When young adults have the mindset that passions develop over time, they're more likely to stick with it even through the "lows" and find ways to maintain their motivation. Teens are at a point in life where they're pruning curiosities and developing passions. If they're told that passion is a magical thing that they'll just happen upon, they'll focus on short-term gratification and drop a new passion at the first obstacle. However, if they understand that passions need maintenance and development, they'll stick with them when things get a little tough or boring and be more focused on the long-term benefits that their passions provide.

Social media is flooded with "find your passion" posts. They tell us that finding our passion will ensure a robust life, full of inspiration and joy. While these posts are well-intentioned and meant to inspire and motivate, they might be doing more harm than good. This type of post solidifies the false belief that having a passion will make life effortless; that once you've found it, you will have limitless motivation, love your life and work, and have a clear path forward. But research shows that it doesn't really work that way. Passions can ebb and flow over time. We might have doubt about our passions or even lose interest periodically. When we instill the belief in teens that they just need to "find" their passion, they'll see the ebbing and flowing as a sign that they're not passionate about the topic at all. It's helpful for parents to start conversations around these kinds of posts and to point out the belief they might be creating in their own teen.

A study done on dancers concluded that there are two types of passion: *harmonious passion* and *obsessive passion* (Padham and Aujla 2014). Harmonious passion occurs when an individual has control over whether to participate in an activity (autonomy), whereas obsessive passion occurs when a person feels their social acceptance and self-esteem are contingent on participating in the activity. If a teen feels they can freely express their opinions and preferences about an activity, they're more likely to develop harmonious passion, which leads to higher self-esteem (Padham and Aujla 2014). On the flip side, a teen is more likely to develop an obsessive passion if they participate in an activity that requires a high degree of specialization, if they feel their participation is extremely important to their parent/guardian, or if they rely heavily on this activity for their identity. Obsessive passion is related to feelings of guilt, anxiety, depression, perfectionism, and disordered eating (Padham and Aujla 2014).

Thus, helping a teen develop their passions is about more than just motivation. Having something(s) they're allowed to choose to become passionate about is good for their psychological well-being. Harmonious passions create positive emotions and moods, help us feel more connected, give meaning to our days and years, help us feel accomplished, and make us engage with life. And a teen with these elements of psychological well-being in place is more likely to have positive outcomes long into adulthood (Kern et al. 2016). Teens with harmonious passions are more likely to turn into adults who have meaningful relationships, develop a sense of purpose and achievement, and are engaged in life. Thus, it's not just about increasing their motivation; it's about giving them a foundation to build a life where they're flourishing and thriving.

Purpose Gives Direction

Purpose is the *why* behind what we do. Individuals who have purpose experience better physical and mental health, tend to live longer, and have more satisfying lives (Burrow, Sumner, and Netter 2014). And like those with passion, people with purpose also tend to show other prosocial tendencies that promote well-being, such as more positive emotions, increased engagement with others, better relationships, and a sense of meaning and accomplishment (Seligman 2011). In addition, teens who have purpose demonstrate safer driving habits, report higher life satisfaction, have a stronger sense of identity, are more psychologically mature, and experience more positive moods in daily life (Burrow, Sumner, and Netter 2014). Yet even though most teens report having a purpose, only 20 percent can identify what their purpose is (Damon 2008).

Purpose differs from passion in that it has direction and motivation. A teen might be very passionate about a musical artist and listen to them constantly, attend their concerts, and watch every video they can find of them, while another teen might be passionate about that same artist, but with the purpose of being just like them and inspiring others to be themselves. As a result, the second teen may take singing lessons or dance classes and work on self-improvement. The first teen is passionate for sure, but lacks the direction, motivation, and ultimately the purpose of the second teen. Still, passions can easily lead a teen to purpose, especially when the teen has control and their self-esteem and social acceptance isn't dependent on the passion.

Purpose is also different from goals, although it may contain goals. Purpose is an "intention to accomplish something that is at once meaningful to the self and consequential to the world beyond the self" (Damon 2008), while goals are steps that can be more quickly accomplished and lead to greater and more desirable results. Max's purpose of designing research projects that will create meaningful change in underserved populations might include goals of graduating from college, getting a master's degree in public policy, or working for a community agency. While his goals are important and will keep him on track, his purpose is truly driving the train. It's also important to note how Damon's definition of purpose includes an intention that is meaningful to the self *and* to the world. When a teen is thinking of an impact beyond their own life, you know they've tapped into their purpose.

Adolescence is prime time for developing purpose, since teens are actively cultivating a sense of self during this time. According to

Erikson's stages of development model, the primary psychological task of adolescence is identity formation (1968). You've likely observed your teen figuring out who they are and who they aren't, what they like and dislike, what's meaningful to them and what's not, and which direction they want to go or avoid. This self-focus and exploration naturally leads to the development of a purpose; however, the naturally narcissistic part of being a teen might keep them a bit more focused on the "meaningful to the self" part and not as much focused on the "world beyond the self" part. In the next chapter, we'll talk about ways to help bridge this gap.

Autonomy Enhances Willingness

Jada is in the tenth grade and has been dancing since the start of middle school. She only started dancing because her parents told her if she had an outside activity where she's getting exercise, she wouldn't have to do a school sport. But now, she loves all her friends at dance. She loves that they don't go to her school, meaning she gets a break from school drama. She also loves that her dance company has allowed the dancers to choose their classes, schedule, recitals, and competitions. She enjoys dance, but she appreciates the flexibility to choose what best fits her each season.

However, when the dance teacher she's been with since she began retired, everything changed. The new dance instructor no longer allows the dancers to choose which dances they want to do. The instructor tells the company that they're going to gain national recognition and start winning at every competition. She creates cohorts where the dancers only practice with each other, so Jada no longer sees most of her friends. Jada enjoys ballet the most and is close to being on pointe. But her new teacher tells her the time has passed and she's switching Jada off ballet and over to contemporary. After practice one day, the teacher goes over the *competitions for the year with Jada's cohort and tells them which ones they'll be attending and what types of dances each will be doing. She ignores the dancers' input completely. Jada leaves practice in tears and goes home to announce to her parents that after three months with the new teacher, she's done with dance and ready to quit.*

Autonomous motivation occurred when Jada was dancing by choice; she wasn't coerced or pressured. Her original instructor focused on the pure enjoyment of dance, allowing Jada to choose for herself along the way. But the new instructor focused on results and took away Jada's choices.

Ryan and Deci found that autonomous motivation is always the more powerful driver of behavior compared with controlled motivation (2000). For teens, this is even truer. Research has found that when parents exert pressure and control over their child, instead of allowing the child the opportunity to take responsibility for their own actions within the value system the parents teach, the child will do the opposite of what the parents want (Grolnick 2003). Additionally, teens are at a developmental stage where they're becoming more independent; when an adult takes away that independence, like Jada's new dance instructor did, most teens will lose motivation for the task completely.

Just to be clear: autonomy does not mean independence; teens can be dependent on others while still being autonomous. Autonomous motivation "emerges from one's sense of self and is accompanied by feelings of willingness and engagement" (Stone, Deci, and Ryan 2008, 4). Encouraging a teen's budding independence and need for autonomous motivation, balanced with parental input and support, might mean giving parameters for expectations and then stepping back so the teen can figure out the details. Jada's parents may have the expectation that she honor commitments and see through any activity she's chosen until the end of the term, and then allow her to figure out how to end her dance career within that framework. Perhaps Jada will decide to decrease the number of classes she takes, only sign up for the required number of competitions, and not do anything extra—or maybe she will talk to her teacher about how she's feeling.

When people have autonomy, they're happier, more creative, and more productive (Stone, Deci, and Ryan 2008). Adults who have more autonomy in their careers tend to also have greater work satisfaction, better work performance, and lower levels of anxiety and depression (Baard, Deci, and Ryan 2004). At school, teens who have autonomy in their learning retain information better and for a longer period (Grolnick 2003). And in sports, teens who can choose their level of participation and set their own goals tend to enjoy the activity more and have greater intrinsic motivation (Grolnick 2003). As a parent, you may have limits on how much autonomy you allow your teen, yet you can still create autonomy-supporting events and environments. For example, you don't have control over what happens in your teen's classrooms or on the soccer field, but at home, you can ensure your teen has a voice in what happens. Even if the teacher gives your teen a list of every detail that needs to go into their presentation, you might encourage them to focus on the aspects that excite them the most or allow them to choose how, when, and where they'll prepare for it.

Mastery Enables Progress

Oliver is a ninth grader just starting high school. He's been looking forward to joining the school's theater program since he was in the seventh grade and first saw one of their productions. When they post auditions for the winter musical, he signs up immediately, despite being an inexperienced singer. He's assigned to be part of the ensemble crew and learns he'll only be in the background in a couple of scenes, so he tells his parents he's going to quit. After his parents point out that he's never worked on his singing and offer some gentle coaxing, he agrees to stick with it and take voice lessons on the weekends. His parents hide their wincing when he practices; but then they notice that they're wincing less over time. Oliver signs up for school choir in the second semester and continues with his private lessons outside of school. His choir teacher begins asking Oliver to demonstrate certain notes in front of the class and gives him a small solo in their spring concert. He also gets a small role in the spring play and finds that he's disappointed it's not a musical. He keeps practicing over the summer by taking lessons and attending musical theater camps, and by winter musical season, he's excited to demonstrate his growth. He lands an actual part; even though it's not huge, he'll get to sing in front of the audience! His parents notice how proud he is of himself and continue to encourage and support him as he develops his voice.

Mastery is making progress in a chosen area. When your teen sees improvement in an area, whether it's academic, athletic, social, creative, or technical, they are likely to do more of that activity. That's because mastery creates momentum—and momentum creates further mastery. As Oliver became a better singer, he wanted to continue in choir and audition for other musicals. His progress motivated him to keep moving forward. In contrast, when mastery is missing and your teen isn't improving, momentum can quickly disappear. Imagine if, after all his hard work, Oliver were put into the ensemble cast again for the next musical. His momentum may have decreased a bit, creating less opportunity to work on his singing. With time, he may have quit singing altogether.

When it comes to mastery, it's not just about progress and momentum though. There needs to be a balance between challenge and skills. If a teen is too challenged, they'll feel overwhelmed, but if they have the skills already, they may be bored. When the challenge/skills balance is in place, there's higher intrinsic motivation and enjoyment of the task (Csíkszentmihályi 1975).

It's not possible for every activity to have a challenge/skills balance. Instead, we can think of it as a balance within the day. If your teen is taking a light academic load, they might need more challenging activities to engage in outside of school. In contrast, if their schedule is academically demanding, they might need to have less-challenging activities outside of school. When teens find challenges within their daily routines, they do more work and feel better while doing it (Hektner and Csíkszentmihályi 1996). If they don't feel challenged in most of what they do each day, they're going to feel bored and unfulfilled and develop poor habits (Hektner and Csíkszentmihályi 1996). We cover how to accomplish this challenge/skills balance in the next chapter.

Like curiosity and passion, mindset also plays a role in mastery. People have beliefs about themselves and what they can accomplish, called self-theories (Dweck 1999). According to Dweck, our self-theories determine how we interpret our experiences and set parameters on what we think we can do (1999). If Oliver thought of himself as "tone deaf" or that people are either born with singing talent or they're not (fixed mindset), he likely wouldn't have pursued singing. His fixed mindset would prevent him from practicing, taking lessons, or even auditioning for the musical. But with his parents' help, he saw singing as a skill that can be developed (growth mindset) and considered auditions, camps, lessons, and choir classes as opportunities to learn and grow. His growth mindset allowed him to keep practicing and trying. A growth mindset puts your teen on the pathway to mastery.

We can't talk about mastery without touching on grit, which is such an important part of motivation that it has its own section in this book. Pursuing mastery takes a mix of hard work, daily grinding, repetition, boredom, and pain. It requires sustained effort over a long time (Ericsson, Krampe, and Tesch-Römer 1993). In fact, no matter the area, whether it's mastery of sports, academics, music, or otherwise, the cycle is the same: intense practice, mundane repetitions, slight progress, more intense effort, more mundane repetitions, slight progress

(Pink 2009). This cycle can be hard on a teen, especially when progress is minimal. This is why it's so important to have the other elements of drive in place, like passion and purpose, so your teen is better equipped to put in the effort.

CHAPTER 3

HELPING YOUR TEEN DEVELOP DRIVE

THIS CHAPTER IS ALL ABOUT action, about the steps that are going to help move your teen forward. We're going to help them become more curious and passionate so they can find purpose. We're also going to cover ways to help them have more autonomy in their lives and build mastery in the areas that are important to them. Please remember this is meant to be fun both for you and your teen! While helping your teen become more motivated might strike you as work, remember that giving them opportunities for growth will help them build self-awareness and a sense of direction. It's going to help improve your communication with them. And you're going to get to know your teen in new ways. If you approach things with a growth mindset, your teen will want to answer your questions, share their thoughts, and do some self-exploration alongside you.

Support Their Curiosity

Curiosity happens naturally when the material is new or interesting. For curiosity to unfold, teens need exposure, space, and time. As mentioned in the previous chapter, when your teen is exploring a new interest, things might arise, change, or end suddenly. One of the biggest issues I see with parents is when they don't recognize that it's curiosity, not a passion (yet), so they push too hard, which can sometimes squash the teen's interest. At the same time, one of the biggest complaints I hear from parents is that their teen never pursues any interest for long. We'll cover both issues.

Give Them Exposure, Space, and Time

It's important that teens have exposure to lots of different activities and interests. They need to stick with the activity a bit to get a sense of how they feel about the activity *and* about themselves doing the activity. Something might look appealing while others are doing it or might sound good in theory, but once they try it, your teen soon realizes it's not a good fit for them. Perhaps your teen wants to join ski club since all their friends are in it, only to find that they don't tolerate the cold well or like how out of control they feel while skiing. Using open-ended questions, you may find that they're not interested enough in skiing to get warmer gear or to take lessons. Exposure to this curiosity allowed them to determine how they felt doing the activity *and* how they felt about themselves while doing it.

Teens also need space to figure things out (mostly) on their own. They need wiggle room to explore a new interest without any input from anyone else. Giving space may mean holding back judgmental comments and biting your tongue when you want so badly to say something. Your teen might tell you they want to try out culinary arts; it's all you can do not to remind them of how they added the cheese powder while the noodles were still in the boiling water. But instead, you hold back the comments and give them space to explore. Whether the new interest leads to a passion or not isn't important; they're getting an opportunity to understand themselves better and to figure out what they like and dislike on their own. Think of these curiosities as data points that their subconscious is tracking and using to calibrate and recalibrate daily. When you allow your teen to safely explore healthy curiosities, you're giving them the gift of self-awareness.

Finally, teens need time to explore their curiosities. Overscheduled and overstimulated teens don't have opportunities to follow a curiosity and see where it takes them; they're far too busy or too drained for that. We want there to be some cushion within their days and weeks. Some teens are pushed to take on too many clubs and activities so it'll look good on their college applications, while others aren't pushed hard enough and end up spending their time scrolling or gaming. We want to find the middle ground here. That might look like telling your teen they must pick one club and one sport per semester (their choice for autonomy's sake!) *and* imposing limits on screen time. This balance gives them time to try out new activities, and without screens filling up their free time, they'll have the opportunity to daydream, feel bored, get creative, and follow roads to nowhere.

Get Curious About Their Curiosities

Most parents want their teen's curiosities to stick and to turn into passion and purpose, especially those interests that will lead to a healthy and productive life. Parents want so badly for their children to have things they enjoy, activities that energize them, and a life full of adventure and excitement. That's why they sometimes push a little too hard when a teen shows interest in something, or pile on the choices so the teen has lots of things to explore. But what I often see happen with parents is that they push so hard, they completely turn off their teen's interest. Or they want so badly for their teen to turn a curiosity into a passion that the parent becomes more invested in the interest than the teen.

When your teen is still exploring a new curiosity, they haven't yet committed. Ask open-ended questions about what they like and dislike, but hold back on sharing your own opinions right now. Make sure they have the exposure, space, and time to follow this curiosity while you occasionally chime in with a question or observation. Maybe your teen is interested in judo and you've paid for a trial month at the local studio. You've given them exposure, so great job already! When you're driving home from class together, casually ask open-ended questions like, "What did you like about tonight's class?" or "What do you enjoy about judo so far?" And if appropriate, offer some observations like, "I've noticed you've been sleeping better since you started taking these classes," or "Seems like you're making new friends there."

Follow their lead. If your teen wants to increase their commitment to a curiosity, allow them. If they pull back a little, allow that as well. Are they taking more or fewer classes? Are they asking to purchase the required attire or complaining about going? Either way, you're letting them dictate the pace of their interest. You can still ask those open-ended questions or make your observations, but you're not telling them what they should or shouldn't be doing. They're figuring that part out on their own.

Cultivate Their Passions

Passions are born out of curiosities that are elevated into enthusiasm and conviction. Before we talk about developing passions, let's do a mindset check. Recall how mindsets can show up during passion. For example, if we teach teens that being passionate about something is supposed to make it easy (fixed mindset), they're more likely to dump that interest when things get hard (or boring). We want to help teens approach passions with the mindset that they require cultivation and maintenance. You can model this growth mindset with your own passions. Perhaps your passion is running and you're training for a half marathon. Training isn't always easy or fun, no matter how much you love running. Talk about the tough days and share what you did to still go on the run regardless. Share what you do to maintain your passion for running, like reading articles about running or being part of a running club.

Harmonious Passion

If you recall, harmonious passion occurs when your teen has control over whether to participate in an activity, whereas obsessive passion occurs when their social acceptance and self-esteem are dependent on participating in the activity. We want your teen to be participating by choice and because they genuinely enjoy the activity. To help with this, point out when you notice your teen enjoying something that they're doing voluntarily. For example, you might see them planning a friend's birthday party and notice how much fun they're having selecting a theme, coordinating colors, and figuring out all the details.

You might point out how much they seem to be enjoying it and ask them what it is about the planning that they like the most.

When it comes to chosen activities that are a bit more structured, like clubs or sports, ask open-ended questions about what they like and don't like, what they're learning, and if they think they'll continue to pursue it. This gives you a chance to see if these passions are harmonious or obsessive. If you hear them saying things like, "People respect me so much more now because I'm on the team," or "It's the only time I feel good about myself," you'll want to talk with them about why it feels this way and offer other ways for them to feel respected or worthy. You can make a mental note that these activities might be falling in the obsessive passion range and keep an eye on things. However, if they tell you, "I love seeing my progress as I get faster and faster," or "I love building robots as a team and how we all have to work together to get it to move," you'll want to support them as they develop and maintain this harmonious passion.

Point out positive changes you notice in them when they participate in the activity, talk about how it's normal for passions to ebb and flow, and provide encouragement for them to keep going. But remember, passions can be numerous, directionless, and without motivation. Your teen might have a diverse set of unrelated passions; if possible, you want them to have time to explore each. Some curiosities may stay in the passion range, while others will turn into a purpose. It needs to be up to the teen to figure this out, not the parent—no matter how badly you may want some passions to dissipate and others to turn into purpose. It needs to come from them, otherwise their passions could become obsessive, fizzle out too early, or lead to them pursuing something that they really don't enjoy.

When They Lack Passion

If you find that your teen has no curiosities, their interests tend to fizzle out before turning into a passion, or they jump from curiosity to curiosity, never letting anything sit long enough to turn into a passion, there are a couple things you can do to guide them. First, have you checked their screen time lately? Remember that the constant stimulation that occurs from scrolling, gaming, and watching videos will make any potential curiosity or passion look boring in comparison. Start with getting them off screens by setting strict limits and providing guidelines on spending time within curiosities that aren't screen related.

Second, do this simple exercise with them to get the passion juices flowing:

PASSION IDENTIFICATION

- Set the timer for 10 minutes. You each write down everything you're passionate about; perhaps protecting wildlife from wildfires or learning how to play the guitar like the musician of your favorite band. Get as specific as possible.

- For the next two weeks, you each spend twenty minutes a day exploring a passion. That might mean reading articles about the topic, practicing or doing the activity, volunteering, watching videos on it (which comes out of their allotted screen time!), etc.

- You each keep a passion journal along the way, taking notes about what you're learning and any insights that arise.

- At the end of the two weeks, talk about what you did, compare notes from your journals, and share what you each learned. Decide which passions you'll each continue to pursue.

Put Words to Their Purpose

Purpose is when your teen has the direction and motivation to complete something that is meaningful to them and will have an impact on the world. It can be huge, like writing a novel, or it might be more like knowing they want to be a writer when they're older. Sometimes it's hard for parents to know when their teen has a purpose, because the teen hasn't yet fully identified it themselves. For instance, a teen who pulls over to help turtles cross the road and is always trying to convince the family that they need to adopt another shelter pet might have a purpose of making the world better for animals, but they haven't yet articulated this. Or perhaps it's hard to identify purpose because they're a bit unorganized and scattered in their passions and life.

To help figure out what their purpose is, to get them on track to developing one, or to help organize their passions into a purpose, do a values audit. I use a variation of this exercise in my coaching sessions with teens.

VALUES AUDIT

- Look at this list of core values with your teen. Discuss what each one means (look up the meanings if you're not sure).

  Authenticity • Achievement • Adventure • Autonomy • Balance • Beauty • Boldness • Compassion • Challenge • Citizenship • Community • Competency • Contribution • Creativity • Curiosity • Determination • Fairness • Faith • Fame • Friendships • Fun • Growth • Honesty • Humor • Influence • Inner Harmony • Justice • Kindness • Knowledge • Leadership • Learning • Love • Loyalty • Meaningful Work • Openness • Optimism • Peace

• Poise • Religion • Reputation • Respect • Responsibility • Security • Self-Respect • Service • Spirituality • Stability • Success • Trustworthiness • Wealth • Wisdom

● Talk about how values are beliefs that define who we are and act as a filter through which we make our choices. Ask them to choose the three values that are most important to them as you do the same.

● If your teen is comfortable doing so, discuss what you each chose as your three core values and why. Ask your teen which of their behaviors are aligned with their values and which pull them away. For example, if they value creativity, have them share their actions that support this value and which actions don't.

● Get curious about how their values are connected to their passions. Ask questions like, "I know how much you love robotics and I see one of your main values is leadership. How do you think those two things could be connected?"

● Point out any connections you notice that they might be missing. Maybe they selected humor as a value and you know they have a passion for performing. Point out how these two things could be connected and suggest auditioning for a funny side role in the next school play or trying out to be the Master of Ceremonies at the next talent show.

● Talk about how their values might be connected to something bigger, something outside of themselves. Perhaps how their value of responsibility would be helpful with climate change. Leave room for discussion to hear how they see their values on a global scale.

Once you've completed this exercise, you and your teen will have a better sense of what their purpose is. It doesn't need to be finely tuned; it's fine if it's more of a direction. The values you identified through this exercise will come in handy when we get into goals.

Sticking with Purpose

Now that you have at least a general sense of what your teen's purpose is, how can you help them stay with it? Even when we have a clearly identified purpose and are fully committed to it, we're going to run into bumps, blocks, and detours along the way. At the age of 12, Jessica Watson's clearly identified purpose was to complete a solo sailing trip around the world, nonstop and unassisted. She told a reporter for the *Los Angeles Times*, "I wanted to challenge myself and achieve something to be proud of. And yes, I wanted to inspire people. I hated being judged by my appearance and other people's expectations of what a 'little girl' was capable of. It's no longer just my dream or voyage" (Burgess 2010). She spent four years working toward her goal and at 16, she completed her dream.

Jessica's clear purpose was meaningful to her and inspirational to others, but she still ran into disinterest, boredom, self-doubt, and lack of clarity during training and the voyage. Her purpose could not have been any more perfect, and she had all the elements of motivation in place (drive, grit, and goals). Yet she still became disinterested and bored at times. She still struggled with self-doubt. And she still had times where she lacked clarity. The things that kept her going in her quest are the very things that will keep your teen on track. The key forces behind maintaining purpose are consistency, support, and focusing on the greater impact. Jessica had to complete trial runs and log nautical miles to gain more experience. She relied on others to build her skills, understand her weaknesses, and encourage and motivate her when needed. Jessica also focused on how she'd inspire other young people to go after their dreams.

Let's look at how this might work for your teen:

★ Consistency includes finding ways to stay on track for the long haul. For the teen destined to write a novel, that might mean writing seven pages a week.

★ Support includes finding others to coach, encourage, cheerlead, or mentor your teen. They might need a writing coach or to join the school's creative writing club.

★ Focusing on the greater impact means figuring out how their purpose will help others or improve the world in some way. Your teen might need reminders of how certain books they've read changed their own life.

Bridging the Gap Between Self and Others

We've talked about how adolescent development includes a bit of self-centeredness, which means their purpose might sometimes focus solely on them and not so much on how it'll help others. While this is normal, it's helpful if we can get them thinking outside of themselves. Thinking of the impact on others will solidify their purpose into something they'll stick with for the long term and help with motivation during the tough times. Jessica didn't just want to sail around the world for herself; she was doing it to inspire others. Focusing on others helped her when she was stuck for days on end without any wind, just drifting in the ocean and questioning everything about her life and herself. When she saw comments on the blog that she updated during the trip, she realized how much her excursion meant to others and knew she couldn't quit.

To bridge the gap from focusing on self to others, help your teen see the potential impact their purpose could have on the world. Maybe your teen who values humor and loves performing only wants to emcee the talent show to be noticed and appreciated. Ask them to consider how their performance might affect others or if there's a way to use their performance for something bigger than themselves. Maybe they realize that they could inspire kids to go outside their comfort zone or that they can use their platform to encourage their peers to do something positive like picking up litter or donating food to the local food pantry.

When your teen is interested in something that has an impact beyond them, encourage them to get involved at a deeper level. This just might help turn the interest into a purpose. If your teen volunteers at a childcare facility serving low-income women, they might realize how hard it is for single moms to manage things when they don't have childcare to rely on. This awareness might prompt questions about economic and gender inequality. Instead of offering your own opinions on these issues, encourage your teen to explore these topics independently and take courses that touch on them. If your teen expresses frustration over how something is being handled by adults, like the school dress code or local curfews, ask who they might speak to about their concerns or how they can get involved to create change.

Give Them Autonomy

As I keep saying, autonomy and motivation go together for everyone, but even more so for teens. Teens need to have opportunities to make mistakes, take responsibility for their actions, and act from their own value system. If a parent coerces, manipulates, or pressures their teen to do something or only do things that fit the parent's value system, the teen won't have those opportunities. This is a hard concept for many parents to accept. Many parents rely on the methods they used when their teen was younger, like control and pressure, and haven't adapted to this new developmental phase of life. But if you don't adapt, you're likely to decrease their motivation, and you might make your relationship with your teen more stressful than it needs to be.

Instead, set clear expectations with guidelines and then step back. Allow your teen to figure out how to operate within the system, even if that means they make a ton of mistakes or screw things up. For school, this means allowing them to work things out directly with the teacher when they miss an assignment or don't understand the directions on a project. Classrooms have guidelines, and your teen needs to learn how to function within them. I often see parents get involved when the threat of a lower grade is looming; however, this is exactly when you need to step back the most. They'll learn far more from that experience than they will from you intervening and protecting them.

Hold Family Meetings

Family meetings are a powerful source of autonomous motivation at home. Family meetings held regularly (weekly, biweekly, or monthly) give everyone in the family a voice in how the system operates. In a home with teens, it's best to create an agenda, take turns leading the meetings, and decide how you'll make tough decisions as a group. When the ages of the kids vary widely, you'll want to consider how to handle everyone's input in a way that seems fair. If you make family meetings a regular part of the schedule, your teen will naturally become more engaged and motivated. When they have a say in things, when they get to help create or change the rules, and when their feedback is valued, they feel empowered.

Use family meetings to create expectations over chores, curfews, and how to treat one another. You'll also want to discuss what to do when someone isn't meeting the expectations or consistently ignores them. What will the consequences be? How do you want to handle this as a family? Decide together and then practice consistency. No one will take the guidelines seriously if they're only sometimes implemented. Let's say everyone is expected to do a chore before heading out for fun on the weekend, but your teen doesn't do it one Saturday. Perhaps the understanding is that when someone skips a chore, they either must return immediately to complete the task, or an extra chore gets added to their list. You can text them their options and allow them to choose. You're letting them take responsibility for their actions without coercion or pressure. They were part of the family meeting where this was decided, have a say in how the family system runs, and ultimately, have some control in the family. With these guidelines in place, there's no need to manipulate, pressure, or offer judgmental comments about their behavior.

Create Autonomy-Supportive Environments

Your teen will care less about things when they have minimal control in the outcome. This isn't a teen thing, it's a human thing: when we don't care, we're less motivated. To help teens get more control in their lives, we want to create autonomy-supportive environments. In sports, this occurs when coaches provide choices, explain reasoning for tasks and limits, base feedback on competence, acknowledge the teen's feelings and perspectives, and provide opportunities for independence while avoiding criticism and rewarding them for doing tasks they find interesting (Coatsworth and Conroy 2009). Here's a breakdown on how each of these could work for you and your teen:

* **Provide choices.** Rather than telling your teen what to do, give them a selection of choices. You might tell them that they must take a language for two years; however, they get to choose which one.

★ **Explain reasoning for tasks and limits.** Whenever you're setting limits or assigning them something to complete, tell them why. Make your rationale clear so that even if they don't agree, they understand your reasons.

★ **Base feedback on competence and avoid personal criticism.** When providing feedback, keep it focused on what skills or abilities are strong or which need to be developed further. Avoid feedback that's critical of them as a person, which includes personality traits. For example, rather than telling your teen they're a mess because their room is, talk about how they need help becoming more organized.

★ **Acknowledge your teen's feelings and perspectives.** This is where those listening skills mentioned in the introduction come in handy! Let them share how they're feeling and thinking, and *listen.* You're not there to argue or prove a point, but rather to understand their perspective better.

★ **Provide opportunities for independence.** Give them space to go out on their own, whether that's talking to the coach or teacher about an issue they're having or going off to sleepaway camp.

★ **Avoid giving tangible rewards for interesting tasks.** This is an instant intrinsic motivational killer. If they're already interested in the task, they don't need an extrinsic reward thrown in to ruin it. Save those for doing the things they despise, like vacuuming the basement.

Build Momentum Toward Mastery

Mastery is such a helpful motivator, but it's also a tricky one for a parent to navigate. It can feel as though you can only do so much to get your teen to make progress, since so much of it falls on them. I often see parents diminish their role here, as though they have absolutely no influence over their teen's progress at all. But there are a few key things parents can do to help their teen make progress and build momentum. Let's look at how you can guide your teen through mastery.

Identify Connections and Process

Your teen has likely mastered a variety of skills throughout their life. From walking and talking to achieving success at a sport, class, or video game, your teen has shown that they know how to go from beginner to expert level. But they might not always see or understand this. They might not realize how far they've come. They also might not see how mastery of a skillset in one area can lead to mastery in another area. When you're able to help your teen make the connection on how skills in one area can help in another area, you're opening a door to a whole new world for them. For example, when your teen decided that they were going to make the cut for orchestra, they had to put in extra practice time, be open to feedback from their teacher, be willing to go outside their comfort zone to play more challenging songs, and exude confidence when playing in front of others. Those are major skills that are going to be handy in all areas of life, not just orchestra.

Your teen also likely has a process for how they master skills. One of my favorite things to do with my coaching clients is to help them understand their process. It could be how they learn a new trick on their snowboard, decrease anxiety before an exam, or approach a new friend group at lunch. There's always a process that we go through first, and I love bringing it to light. And once your teen understands their process, they can apply it to other things. Plus, they learn that they can create a process for most situations. Teens love breaking down their process almost as much as I love helping them do it. They feel empowered when they realize that they've had what they needed all along, right there inside of them.

Figuring out the skills required to help them make connections and deciphering their process so they can apply it to other areas go together well. Let's look at how you can guide them through this. Use this exercise when they're struggling and filled with self-doubt and need support to stay on track. You can also use these prompts before they've begun and are excited to try something new.

ASSESSING THEIR PROCESS

- **Consider a skill that they've come a long way in developing.** They don't need to be an expert, but they've made some serious progress. Encourage them to write or talk about it by asking them to recall what it was like to be a beginner. How did it feel? What did they have to learn? How did they overcome obstacles?

- **Help them identify the skills required.** What did they have to do to improve? Get as specific as possible. For example, when learning a new bike trick, they had to learn breathing exercises to manage stress when going down larger slopes, how to take feedback without getting defensive, and how to ask for help when in need of extra support or guidance.

- **Ask them how they might use each skill in areas completely different from the one they mastered.** How do these different skills help in other areas of life? How can they be applied elsewhere? You might ask the biker, for instance, how these skills will help when giving a presentation at school.

- **Help them break down their process.** What steps did they need to go through to master the skill? Don't let them skip over the easy steps either. The biker likely had to break the trick apart into smaller steps, practice each small step repeatedly, put the whole trick together to do on an air bag, watch videos of themselves to correct errors, talk to more advanced riders for advice, work on thought control so they didn't get down on themselves, do visualizations, and so on.

- **Look at how their process can help with further mastery development.** How would they change this process for more complex tasks? What would they leave the same? How could this process help them with something else they're currently trying to master?

Promote a Challenge/Skills Balance

Imagine a seesaw where you've got anxiety on one side and boredom on the other. When it comes to mastery, we want the seesaw balanced. If it's too heavy on the side of anxiety, your teen will get overwhelmed and is more likely to give up. If it's too heavy on the side of boredom, they'll become apathetic and won't want to do it. But if the seesaw sits in that sweet spot of perfect balance, your teen will feel momentum, see their progress, and be motivated to keep going. It's a magical place to be and isn't as hard to get to as you might think. It's just a matter of helping your teen understand their limits and strengths.

First, talk to your teen about the challenge/skills balance. I've found that many are unaware of this concept, but once they learn about it, they start to monitor where they are with things. They'll say things like, "I'm falling into anxiety, this is too far outside my skillset right now," or "I'm so bored, this is way too easy for me." This is great self-awareness, and we want to foster it when it pops up. Second, gently point out your own observations when you notice the seesaw losing balance. This might sound like, "You seem really stressed out the last couple of days. Is it possible you're overwhelmed with how much new choreography you're having to learn right now at dance?" or "I've noticed that you're sleeping more than usual lately and don't seem as interested in tennis. Do you think you're bored now that the coach has you practicing with younger players?"

Once your teen has become more familiar with the challenge/skills balance, start to check in with them routinely and get their own self-assessment. Ask them where they fall on the seesaw for certain activities or even with their daily schedule. Where do they feel overwhelmed? Where do they feel bored? Help them brainstorm ways to find the middle ground. For a specific activity, this might look like asking the coach for more challenging drills when bored or for guidance when overwhelmed. When it comes to their daily schedule, it might mean figuring out ways to balance out their days or weeks. For instance, dispersing the hard things throughout the week and making sure there's time for both challenging and easy within each day.

CHAPTER 4

WHAT IS GRIT?

Lauren is a tenth grader who learned about coding and app creating during a robotics after-school club. She worked on a team that competed with others in coding battles and learned how to make her own artificial intelligence (AI) bot. She was most interested when the club spent time designing their own apps and learned some of the basic skills needed for creating their own. When the club ended, she told her parents about the app she was determined to make and showed them her outline of all its functions. She told everyone how her app was going to change how teens selected and applied to college. She used the skills and knowledge she gained at the club to begin setting it up. When she ran into problems, she googled for solutions and was able to overcome some of the issues, but began to realize that her initial app design was likely too complex for her skills. She signed up for a coding class and immediately told her teacher about her app.

At the start of the semester, she focused on building it, but soon found other things that were a bit easier and more fun for her, like creating silly websites for fictious businesses she and her friends laughed over. She'd work on the app for a bit, but as soon as she became stuck, she'd switch to a completely different project. She complained to her teacher that there were too many steps needed and that this was way more time-consuming than she thought it'd be. By the end of the semester, she was mostly goofing around in class and playing the simple video games her peers designed during their work time. When her parents asked about the app, she told them it was too hard to create, and she didn't care that much about it anymore anyway.

GRIT IS OUR PERSEVERANCE TO stick with things, even when they become difficult or boring. Angela Duckworth has spent years researching what makes a person *gritty* and defines it as "a combination of passion and perseverance for a singularly important goal" (Duckworth 2016). It consists of perseverance of effort, consistency of interest, goal attainment, and passion (Duckworth and Yeager 2015). Perseverance of effort (being able to exert long-lasting effort) and consistency of interest (the ability to maintain a steadfast interest in a task) are the two distinct parameters for grit that need to be present.

Lauren had passion initially and some sense of a goal, but her interest and effort didn't hold up over time. Perhaps her passion was fleeting or her goal wasn't grounded in purpose. Or maybe she hasn't yet learned perseverance—how to stick with things when they become more challenging. If she had maintained her interest and passion AND was willing to put in consistent effort, she would have stuck with her app development, learned more skills, and continued solving the problems that popped up. She might have even ended up creating her app. But as her example shows, when we lack committed interest or enduring effort, it's easy to find other things to do, become distracted, or go off track.

Grit builds individual traits like self-regulation, self-control, and task persistence (Hwang and Nam 2021). Self-regulation—the ability to control thoughts, emotions, and behaviors—enables your teen to exert long-lasting effort. Self-control—the ability to resist temptations in pursuit of long-term gains—allows them to maintain steadfast interest. And task persistence—staying with a job already started—allows your teen to stick with all the small steps that go into a big goal. These traits will help your teen be successful in any area of life. When your teen builds grit, they're strengthening these traits. If your teen already has strong self-regulation, self-control, or task persistence, it'll be easier for them to be gritty. Chances are though, like most teens, they're seriously lacking in one, two, or all three of the areas. We'll get them on track so they can develop them along the way.

Grit Is Fuel

Grit fuels sustained action over an extended period, even when adversity is present (Good Life Project). Specifically, grit is *long-term* passion and *long-term* perseverance. Grit keeps your teen loyal to their passions and commitments even when their friends lose interest in a shared passion, they run into challenges or setbacks, or they experience long plateaus with minimal progress. Grit is the fuel that keeps the engine running. We can have all the drive in the world and the clearest of goals, but if we don't have interest and perseverance for the long haul, we're not going to accomplish much. Consider how easy it was for Lauren's interest in her app to diminish when she ran into roadblocks, and how she decided that creating the app required too much time or too many steps. Without long-lasting interest and perseverance, she lost steam and couldn't keep moving forward.

Grit can be physical or mental. Think of the physical grit a swimmer needs to swim for hours each week. They must push themselves in practices and races, going past what they previously could do. Think of the mental grit a person needs to complete a 1,000-piece puzzle and how drained they may get, but they still stay focused on completion. Think of a marathon runner who needs both physical and mental grit to train and complete their lengthy run.

Of course, no one has grit all the time, physical or mental. We'd burn ourselves out if we did! While we may not have physical or mental grit every moment of every day, it's a tendency that energizes us to keep working toward the things we're most passionate about. As Duckworth said in her TED Talk, "Grit is living life like it's a marathon, not a sprint" (2013).

To get more fuel in the tank, we need to have interest, deliberate practice, purpose, and hope. An amateur snowboarder who wants to improve and go pro will have an easier time sticking with the hard work required during the off-season (interest). A chess player who keeps looking for ways to optimize their improvement is much more likely to be gritty (deliberate practice). The aspiring filmmaker who relies on their vision of creating something that will inspire others is able to continue moving forward (purpose). The teen who dreams of becoming a rapper and hangs pictures of their musical idols on their walls to help them feel inspired stays on track (hope). We'll cover ways to instill interest, deliberate practice, purpose, and hope in your teen in chapter 6.

Does your teen put in effort on things they're interested in? Do they show a consistent interest in any activity or idea? Do they have a vision or goal that they're working toward? Do they have a passion for something that's been with them for a few months or more?

ASSESSING GRIT

It's invaluable to know where you fall on the grit spectrum as you're helping your teen build it themselves. Answer the questions below first for yourself, and be as honest as you can. Then either have your teen answer the questions or answer for them. If you need to build a bit of grit in yourself and your teen simultaneously, I want you to know that now. Or if you're super gritty but your teen isn't, this is good to know as well.

Rate each statement as true or false:

- I tend to quit easily when I encounter a challenge.

- I change my goals frequently.

- I only work hard on the things I'm passionate about or extremely interested in.

- When working toward a goal or something impor- tant to me, I typically start off strong but then fizzle out with time.

- I have lots of things I'm interested in and jump around between them.

If you or your teen answered "true" to more than one state- ment, you or they might be lacking in grit right now. Please keep in mind, this is a basic screening tool; you're just getting a general idea of how gritty they are.

If you answered "true" to most of those statements, don't freak out. We'll cover ways to build and increase grit in the fol- lowing chapters. Just remember which statements you answered with a hard-and-fast "true." You'll want to keep those in mind as you learn more about grit. They'll help you know which areas to pay close attention to so you have the right tools in your toolbox.

Grit Can Be Learned

Behavior genetics studies show that personality is only 40 percent genetic; the remaining 60 percent comes from environmental influ- ences (Vukasović and Bratko 2015). This means that, while some aspects of your teen's personality are stable and will not change over time, most of their personality can be shaped and cultivated. Environmental influences forming your teen's personality include things like friends, teachers, coaches, school, and teams, as well as the information they consume from social media, television, books, movies, video games, and the internet in general. If your personality includes a ton of grit but you can't figure out why your teen isn't following in your footsteps, look at their environmental influences. They're getting more of their personality traits from those things than they are from you.

Environmental influences are particularly important to pay attention to during adolescence since this is a period of increased independence. Most teens want more time away from their family, which means more time with others or more time alone consuming information. I've worked with lots of teens who talk about characters in books or from shows as if they were real. They'll tell me all about the character's life and their daily dramas. They're telling me about it because this character is influencing them—how they think, how they feel, and how they behave. This character is giving them a chance to experience a life different from their own and see how various elements fit. And the teen will ultimately decide which parts to keep and which ones to let go. I like to help the teen dissect what they like and dislike about the character and their life, so their choices about what to keep are more intentional and conscious.

Pay attention to who they're spending time with and the information they're consuming. See if you notice any commonalties such as shared interests within a friend group, themes in shows or movies, genres of books, or the type of teacher or coach your teen prefers. When you find these commonalities, it's a window into your teen's biggest influences and a chance to see the very things that could be shaping their personality. Ask yourself what kind of messages your teen is getting from their favorite book or teacher. And since we're talking about grit here, look for who shows long-lasting passion and long-lasting perseverance. Which movie character sticks with things, no matter how hard it gets? Which friend has stayed with the same passion for years?

Even if your teen is lacking grit now, it's a trait that can change over time and with life experience (Hoeschler, Backes-Gellner, and Balestra 2018). Remember, they're at peak identity-formation time right now and their current personality is likely to shift and evolve even more than it already has. Perhaps they need more supports in place like deliberate practice or purpose. Or maybe they need a gradual increase in expectations, so they have more opportunity to be gritty. Or possibly a change in some of their environmental influences where they're exposed to more people or movies with grit. (We'll cover how to do all these things in chapter 6.) Think of grit as a muscle they're building. Even if it's weak now, it can get stronger with time and work. In fact, grit is a trait that continues to develop beyond adolescence and well into adulthood.

If your teen shows a gritty personality now, you can help build upon it so they become even grittier. Help them break down ambitious goals into smaller ones so it's easier to stay on track with the things that matter most to them. Have them practice using the grit-building skills you're learning here on things that aren't quite as meaningful to them. This will help them get used to being gritty across the board and not just on the things they're passionate about.

There isn't a huge downside to being gritty, and there's no such thing as having too much grit, but there are a few things to look out for in your super-gritty teen. You want to make sure they don't become inflexible in their quest to achieve and ignore other options. For example, perhaps they're so focused on getting a particular part in the play that they ignore an opportunity to try out set design. You'll also want to make sure they aren't just sticking with something because of the time or effort invested so far. Perhaps they don't want to change jobs because they've already gone through certification and training before they found something different that's a better fit. If your teen is extremely ambitious and you're worried about them being too gritty, help them consider various options on their path forward and do frequent check-ins to help them make the best decisions possible.

Grit Can Be Taught

Have you ever heard the word *sisu*? It's a Finnish term that goes back more than 500 years; it essentially means mental fortitude and is a huge part of Finnish culture. For example, Finnish kiddos ride their bikes or walk to school most days of the year, no matter the weather—in a country where the winter months have an average daily temperature just above freezing. Winter swimming is also a popular pastime in Finland, and it's common to find lakes where people have broken through the ice and dropped in rope ladders to create accessible swimming holes. But *sisu* isn't just about cold exposure. It's about enduring hardship and tapping into internal energy reserves to overcome adversities and discomfort (Pantzar 2022). And while *sisu* encompasses many other psychological qualities and components, grit is a big part of it.

I'm not saying we should force kids to walk to school when the weather is awful or that we should all go jump in the lake during winter, but I do think there's something to be learned from a culture that embraces grit. We want teens who can tolerate discomfort and know how to manage adversity. Instead, I often see adults rush in to rescue—robbing that teen of an opportunity to develop grit. When we hand them a device because the car ride is long, we're telling them they're incapable of entertaining themselves. When we rush to fix a problem they're struggling with, we're sending a clear message that they're not capable enough to fix it themselves. And when they tell us of a big goal or dream they have and we suggest something smaller and more attainable instead, we're letting them know that we don't actually think they can achieve anything more.

I see it happen a lot: the teen sets high expectations of what they want to achieve but the parent says, "Hmmmm…why don't you shoot for this smaller thing instead…?" When we have low expectations of what a teen is capable of, most teens are going to meet us there. If I think my teen client can't become a musician, I'll encourage them to apply for other jobs, pursue other passions, and focus on other things. My client will pick up on my obvious lack of belief and change their own behaviors. They'll likely play music less often, drift among various passions, and attempt to pursue other goals, but probably without the conviction they would have if they were pursuing music. My low expectations just caused this teen to change course completely.

Consider what would happen if I were to fully believe my client could reach their goal and just needed some support and guidance to get there. What would be different? I'd help them identify the steps they need to take, figure out where they struggle to stay on track, and create a plan for them to follow. My client sees that I think they're capable, which helps them believe it for themselves. They have a way forward. And if they go off course a bit, I'd help them figure out why and what they need to do differently when they get back on track. (This last part is grit.) I'm helping them build a belief in themselves that they can do hard things, know how to manage challenges, and can figure out how to correct course when needed. Isn't that beautiful?

Teaching your teen about grit isn't about showing them statistics and giving them a quiz. Teaching your teen grit happens through life. It happens when you let them struggle to solve a problem with a difficult teacher. It occurs when you allow them to feel uncomfortable at a banquet dinner where they don't know anyone and you're holding their phone for the night. It happens when you set high expectations for what they can accomplish in life and you assume they'll figure it out. And it also happens when you accept the expectations they've set for themselves and you allow them to fail painfully along the way, without suggesting they lower the bar they've set.

Just as Finnish people incorporate grit into their culture through *sisu*, you can incorporate it into your family culture through your own version. By allowing your teen to struggle, fail, and fix repeatedly, you're teaching grit and they're building their grit muscle.

I can hear some parents yelling right now: "My teen won't ever get to the fix part! They'll just struggle and fail over and over!" And here's exactly what I tell the parents I work with: That's okay. Let them struggle and fail. Help them reflect on what worked or didn't work and allow them to learn from their mistakes, even if it's at a pace slower than what you'd prefer. This is how grit works. It has to come from our own struggles. We literally cannot develop grit from watching others struggle or from having someone protect us from struggling. *Your teen must struggle to develop grit.*

A Gritty Mindset Matters

This seems like a good time to bring up mindset again, for two reasons. We need to discuss *your* mindset when it comes to grit, and we need to talk about the role of mindset in grit overall. When you read "*Your teen must struggle to develop grit,*" what came up for you? What thoughts did you have? What emotions showed up? No thought or feeling is wrong, but I want you to be aware of them, because those thoughts and feelings will impact how well you're going to tolerate your teen struggling. Some parents struggled so much themselves growing up that they want to protect their child from ever having to do the same. Other parents still see their teen as the young, incapable baby they once were and can't let go of helping. Some parents push their teens so hard that they completely turn their teen off from pushing themselves. Where do you fall? Which story most closely matches your own?

Whatever your mindset about letting your teen struggle, now is a good time to see where you need to shift and change. Where can you allow your teen to grapple a bit more? Where can you back off? Where do you need to push a bit harder? Focus your own mindset on how growing grit is good for your teen and how you want them to be able to handle hard things in life. You want your teen to fail *now*, when they're under your roof and supervision, so you can help guide and support them as they navigate their way through it. You do not want their first major failure to occur when they're living on their own, far from home. They won't know what to do or how to handle it. And you want your teen to learn how to handle adversity now because it's inevitable. Adversity is a part of life, and no matter how wonderful you are at protecting them, you can't protect them from everything. They're going to have to learn eventually—wouldn't you rather they learn it now when you're there to keep an eye on things?

If you recall, a fixed mindset can create the false belief that passions involve effortless fun and that you don't need to work to maintain or cultivate them. But a growth mindset creates the more accurate belief that passions will ebb and flow, won't always be easy or fun, and require some maintenance to keep going. Growth and fixed mindsets affect grit too. If a teen thinks their intelligence or talents can improve and grow over time and with hard work (growth mindset), they're likely to stick with things and be gritty. When a teen thinks, "This is just how I am" (fixed mindset), they're less likely to put in effort to change and will be less gritty.

As we're helping our teens increase their grit, we need to make sure we're working on mindset at the same time. We want teens to know how much control they have over their results. By focusing on where they can grow and develop, they can improve their outcome. I often hear teens say things like, "This isn't natural for me," or "I'm not good enough" when they reach a roadblock or setback. This fixed mindset becomes a whole new roadblock that must be overcome before the actual problem can be addressed. I find that when I gently point out their fixed mindset and ask them to come up with a different way to think about their abilities, they're able to change things around pretty quickly. Usually, this is because we've been working on mindset a lot leading up to this. At home, if you make mindset a regular part of conversation and family culture, your teen will be better able to identify when they've fallen into a fixed mindset trap. We'll cover how to do this in chapter 6.

If you need to build grit in both yourself and your teen simultaneously, you might want to share with your teen what you're learning about grit and how it applies to both of you. Remember, they learn best through modeling, so you'll have the perfect opportunity to do that here! But if you find that you're grittier than your teen, you'll want to focus on all the techniques in the next chapters.

CHAPTER 5

A DEEPER DIVE INTO GRIT

NOW THAT YOU'VE GOT A basic understanding of what grit is, let's go even deeper. We're more inspired to stay on course when we understand the *why* behind things (our purpose). And I really want to increase your motivation to get your teen grittier. Our teens are struggling in this department in major ways. Today's teens are less likely to go out without their parents, drive, work, or do other typical adolescent activities (Twenge 2017). In the last chapter, I mentioned how teens need to struggle to develop grit. If they're not going out without their parents or participating in typical teen activities, where will they develop their grit? Not while scrolling on their phones or with you helping them through their homework, that's for sure. But before we get into that further, let's consider a bit of history.

The importance of grit was identified as far back as 1892, although it wasn't labeled as such back then (Duckworth et al. 2007). Researchers who looked at highly successful people across a variety of professions found that ability alone wasn't enough to ensure their success. True, individuals needed some level of ability, but they also needed zeal and the capacity to put in lots of work. In the mid-1900s, similar conclusions were reached by other researchers who again looked at successful people across different careers, this time focusing on intelligence. They found that when intelligence was similar, a person's persistence of effort was one variable that predicted achievement. And in 1994, yet another study concluded that innate talent or ability isn't as important as the amount and type of practice a person puts into their work (Duckworth et al. 2007).

Your teen can be as smart, capable, or naturally gifted as the peer sitting next to them in science class, but if they lack grit and the other teen has it, they likely won't be as successful. Grit could be the very thing that sets them apart, the very thing that sets them up for a long-term achievement. The beauty of grit is that it's not only about learning in school; it helps your teen stick with long-term pursuits as well.

Essentially, when your teen is building grit, they're focusing on self-control for the task at hand AND for pursuing a long-term aim. Individuals high in grit set long-term goals and will not go off course, even when they don't receive positive feedback (Duckworth et al. 2007). When your teen has grit, they'll stick with their dream, even if it doesn't get them likes on social media.

Teens Need More Grit

Teens who lack the ability to stick with effort and hard work are going to switch from one goal to the next, never reaching what they set out to achieve. Even when they're working toward their big goals or purpose (chapter 7), they won't put in the extra effort and, instead, may think they're bad at it or it's not truly what they're meant to do. They won't understand that it's normal to have to put in work to excel. And then it becomes a vicious cycle: they don't put in the necessary work to achieve their goal so they don't make progress, which leads to them thinking they're not capable of doing well, so they don't put in the necessary work on the next area of pursuit, and on and on it goes. In contrast, a gritty teen will put in effort over a long period of time, which eventually will lead to some sort of progress. The progress creates momentum to keep going and feeds the belief in themselves that they're capable. They continue on their path forward.

Additionally, teens who don't have the mental fortitude to pursue a goal or aim without constant positive feedback are going to be more psychologically fragile. They're not going to know how to handle a roadblock or detour and may end up quitting instead. They won't know what to do when adversity hits and might leave their dreams behind. They won't know how to respond when they encounter plateaus in progress or don't get their desired results; they may decide it's a sign they're not on the right path. A gritty teen will remain focused on their mental aim both when they get positive feedback from others and when they encounter a setback. They find ways around barriers; even though they might flounder a bit, they're committed to staying with their vision and will get back on course.

I often start working with teens after they've given up on something big. They had a big dream, like becoming popular or staying on top of their schoolwork all semester, but quit when they don't see their follower count growing or they realize they missed a few assignments. Their parents are frustrated, because this isn't the first time they've seen their teen retreat when things haven't worked out for them. As we figure out their passions and purpose so we can create new goals, the teen inevitably shares with me all the times they've quit on their plans. They lay it all out in front of me as if it's evidence that we should just stop now. I teach them about grit and how their evidence shows they need growth in this area. I make it simple and tell them it's just a trait we need to build and make stronger. That doesn't mean they're a weak person or can't accomplish things.

I also have a front row seat for observing teens' thoughts when they don't reach the next level or attain the thing they've been working so hard to get. I hear them marvel at how much easier it is for everyone else, how it must be a sign to quit, and how they fail at everything. I let them vent for a moment before asking them to consider their purpose, their *why* behind their actions. I help them get back in touch with their initial reason for wanting this next step to begin with before diving into all the other times they've struggled in their life. We identify what they did to deal with each barrier so they can realize how challenges are normal and not a sign that they should quit. Teens often forget their previous setbacks and that they have demonstrated the inner resources to keep going forward before. When they're able to get back on track, they're developing the skill of a lifetime. The skill of doing hard things. The skill of grit.

Goals Help Create Grit

A teen who is dedicated to a specific goal tends to show more grit (Tang et al. 2019). In fact, when your teen is pursuing something extremely intense and challenging, their commitment to reaching that goal is the single best predictor as to whether they'll stick with it or abandon it (Locke and Latham 2002). Their commitment is more important than any feedback or incentives they might receive. Actress Kristen Wiig spent ten-plus years going to auditions while working all kinds of odd jobs to support herself (Stern 2021). She returned to her hometown to visit childhood friends during this period and noticed how all her friends were busy in their chosen careers and how many had homes, partners, and children. When asked by her friends how her own acting career was going, all she could do was let them know she was getting auditions. While Kristen demonstrated high grit, she most certainly wasn't getting positive feedback or any sort of incentive to keep her going. But her commitment to becoming an actress allowed her to remain laser-focused on her dream and to stay persistent in her effort.

Goal commitment is a bit of a balancing act in adolescence. We want our teens to recognize dead-end pursuits so they can move on to more promising ways forward. At the same time, we know that it takes years of deliberate practice to become excellent at their chosen craft. When teens constantly shift goals and plans or when they find themselves starting over repeatedly, they're learning what doesn't work. But when they take the time to create goals that are based in purpose, they'll find they want to be committed to those goals. They're getting the opportunity to develop grit as they face the monotonous repetition, continuous practice, and slow progress that goes along with goal achievement. Learning how to balance letting go of dead-end pursuits with the necessary practice required for honing a skill takes lived experience and a certain level of maturity. This means your teen needs to go through shifting goals and plans for a while to get that experience. Remember, while they are learning from their mistakes, their brain is continuing to develop; eventually, experience and maturity will make them capable of sticking with long-term goals and grit.

I know this is a tough balancing act to achieve—I'm basically asking you to hold two opposing ideas in mind at the same time. You may be thinking, "This makes no sense! How am I supposed to get them to let go of dead-end pursuits AND put in tons of practice and effort so they can hone a skill?! How is this possible?!" I hear you. I work with teens, remember? I have to hold these two opposing ideas in mind every day. I help teens and their parents navigate this tricky area; I understand how confusing it can be.

Let's start by defining dead-end pursuits as the things your teen isn't that curious about, doesn't have much passion for, or doesn't see as aligned with purpose. Now think of them putting in practice and effort on something they've shown curiosity in, have passion for, or have identified with purpose. As you've learned, it's normal and expected that curiosities will change (remember, by their very definition, curiosities arise and end abruptly). Your teen will change what they're curious about; however, encouraging exploration will help turn some curiosities into passions. Passions occur when your teen is enthusiastic about something, but lacks direction. We're teaching them that passions must be cultivated and encouraging them to put in effort to see which passion holds and will turn into purpose. Remember, purpose is when they have their reason *why* and a mental goal or aim that they're striving toward.

This is where the fun stuff happens. Once we've helped them through curiosities and passions to purpose, they're ready to hone their skills. *This* is where we want them to put in effort and deliberate practice on their chosen craft. And this is where we help them let go of some dead-end pursuits—things that they're not really that interested in or passionate about, or aren't aligned with their purpose. We're helping them turn their purpose into goals, which you'll learn how to do in the next section. Goal commitment creates grit. Show me a teen with a clear goal and I'll show you a teen with serious grit.

I want you to understand grit and its importance before we get into goals, for a couple of reasons. First, I want *you* to have the grit to help your teen create goals, since it can be a tedious process. Second, I want you to really get the purpose of grit and why your teen will need it before you help them create goals. Because if they've got a bit of grit in place before they've even created their goals, think of how much further they'll go!

Purpose over Pleasure

People with grit are more likely to pursue happiness through engagement and meaning, while less gritty individuals tend to pursue happiness via pleasure (Von Culin, Tsukayama, and Duckworth 2014). In other words, people who score high in grit will focus on attention-absorbing activities like reading a good book or going on a bike ride to feel happy. Additionally, gritty people choose activities that serve a higher goal or aim outside of themselves, like creating a supportive community or fighting social injustices. Individuals who score lower in grit tend to rely on things that bring immediate pleasure, like drinking alcohol or binge-watching a series. These individuals are focused more on activities that provide short-term gratification and immediate feel-good sensations.

Grit requires more work up front; however, it creates better benefits in the end. When your teen puts in hard work to get a spot on the school yearbook team, they're going to feel significantly better than when they've spent time online shopping. Or when your teen shows up every Saturday morning to clean out the horse stalls at the nearby animal rescue, they're going to feel happier than if they'd just slept in those days. Every time your teen chooses an activity that they're engaged in over something that will bring immediate pleasure, they're demonstrating grit. Every time they put in effort on something outside of themselves instead of taking the easy route, they're showing you their mental strength.

Not only is your teen going to feel better for putting in effort, they're also much more likely to remember the experience. We remember the times we worked hard much better than the times we loafed. Such positive memories enhance life experience by giving meaning and breaking up the monotony of daily tasks. One of my favorite exercises to do with teens is to have them write down everything they did in the last twenty-four hours and rate each activity on how aligned it was with their goals or future self. As we reflect on their list, they realize how difficult it was to remember the easy stuff. They can easily recall the tasks where they worked hard or went outside their comfort zone, but not the times they scrolled on their phone out of pure boredom.

Developing a life purpose can increase your teen's grit (Hill, Burrow, and Bronk 2016). When your teen has cultivated a passion into a purpose, they're more likely to stick with it and even choose it over more immediately pleasurable activities. While a true life purpose will extend beyond the self, it's fine if your teen's isn't there yet. If their life purpose is more self-focused—perhaps about college admissions, landing a part in the school play, playing in a band, or saving money so they can buy a car—they still have a mental goal or aim that they're working toward. As they develop a stronger sense of self, they'll be ready to think about how their purpose can extend beyond their own needs and wants.

If you find that your teen is focused on short-term gratification and you're unable to get them to engage in meaningful activities without a fight, the next chapter is for you. Or if you think your teen's life purpose is superficial and won't get them far, I've got some action steps coming your way on this very topic. In the meantime, share this information with your teen! Let them know how focusing on long-term purpose over immediate pleasure can help them become grittier—and happier.

Research shows that when teens learn about how their brains work, they're willing to create change. Just remember to do it in a way that's nonjudgmental. Perhaps during your next car ride, you ask them if they've learned anything new or interesting lately. Once they've shared, take your turn and say, "I'm learning about grit and how having a life purpose can help us become grittier." Tell them how doing things that benefit us in the long-run are better for us than doing something that only brings immediate pleasure, like how choosing veggies at dinner is better than skipping them and going straight to dessert. Share it in a way that's nonthreatening, keep it brief, and speak in the first person (we, us) rather than second person (you).

"Becoming" Rather Than "Being"

When teens believe they can develop abilities, skills, and traits, they're much more likely to put in effort toward their goal. This growth mindset allows them to focus on mastery and progress even under great difficulty or failure. And when they do fail, the teens who attribute their lack of success to effort or strategy, rather than ability, tend to persist instead of quitting (Dweck 1986). When Michael Jordan was placed on the high school junior varsity basketball team instead of the varsity team he tried out for, he focused on increasing his practice and effort. Imagine if he had thought being put on the JV squad meant he wasn't a good player? He would've likely missed out on the crucial learning and training he needed to improve.

When teens learn about neuroplasticity—how the brain has a life-long ability to rewire and change itself in response to learning and experience—they're more likely to view their intelligence and abilities as things that can be improved (Tirri and Kujala 2016). Essentially, just learning about mindset changes our mindset! Students who learn about neuroplasticity and growth mindsets tend to have higher academic achievement and motivation in the classroom (Blackwell, Trzesniewski, and Dweck 2007). These findings are exciting for your teen (and for us as adults!). They mean that we're capable of improving at anything if we understand that it just takes learning and experience (practice). Now this doesn't mean that any one of us could become the next Michael Jordan if we only put in effort and work, but it does mean that we can significantly improve our basketball skills with some coaching and lots of time on the court.

Additionally, teens with a growth mindset are focused on "becoming" rather than "being." For example, a teen who's focusing on *becoming smarter* rather than *being smart* will be more resilient when they receive a low grade from a teacher or if a peer makes negative comments about their skills or abilities. Such a teen will be more likely to seek out challenging learning opportunities. They don't view themselves or their abilities as a finished product, which opens them up to growth and development. The teen who is focused on being smart is more likely to be knocked down by negative comments and will avoid challenging themselves. Their mindset creates an identity that "I'm smart," and anything that doesn't fit that criterion, like a low score on a test, will crush them. They may avoid opportunities that don't demonstrate how smart they are and miss out on further growth. Maybe they have a chance to go out for the Science Olympiad team, but they're not as confident in science as other academic areas, so they end up saying no to the opportunity because it doesn't fit their identity of being smart.

Not only does mindset help develop and maintain grit, but it also literally changes neural processes in our brains (Tirri and Kujala 2016). Brain researchers have examined behavioral responses using electro-physiological monitoring to see how individuals detect and respond to mistakes. In multiple studies, they've found that individuals with a growth mindset have different neural reactivity to mistakes. Growth-mindset individuals are incredible at detecting their own mistakes when compared with fixed mindset folks. Not only that, but those with a growth mindset rebound from their mistakes much more quickly and accurately (Tirri and Kujala 2016). In other words, when we understand that our brains can adapt, rewire, and change with effort and practice, we're better at realizing when we've made mistakes and will correct them with greater accuracy than if we believe that we can't improve with effort and practice.

Children develop their mindset early in life at home and school. If they're constantly exposed to environments that praise talent over improvement, they're more likely to believe "This is just how I am." For instance, maybe they had a grandparent who compared all the grandchildren to one another, emphasizing who was naturally good at one thing over another. Additionally, teens who were taught to focus on results and that failure is bad will have more of a fixed mindset. Perhaps your teen went to a school that emphasized high grades and grade point average above all else, and the teachers never noticed who put in extra effort to make sense of difficult material or demonstrated progress throughout the semester. If this is the case with your teen, it's not too late to turn things around. In fact, if this is the case with *you*, it's not too late to turn things around! Neuroplasticity happens throughout our lives; we're all capable of growth and change, no matter our age or stage of life.

We'll dive into mindset-changing action steps in the next chapter, as well as tangible things to do with your teen, but I challenge you to start now. Start noticing where a fixed mindset shows up for *you*. Where do *you* prioritize end results over learning? When do *you* praise talent over effort? When do *you* make fun of or criticize others' failures? As you're collecting your observations, be kind to yourself. These questions aren't meant to make you feel bad or that you're failing at parenting. They're meant to bring awareness to areas of life where you may have a fixed mindset so you can see how you might be transferring those beliefs onto your teen. And when you become more aware, your brain rewires and changes itself as well. Everyone wins!

CHAPTER 6

HELPING YOUR TEEN BECOME GRITTY

GRIT IS A SKILL THAT can be enhanced in adolescence through the very things you'll be learning in this chapter, and grit continues to develop into adulthood. Additionally, grit is only *partially* genetic but *largely* affected by the environment (Hwang and Nam 2021). In other words, when we change what's around them, we can increase your teen's grit. When you help your teen build grit, they learn that putting in effort pays off. They see how it helps to solidify their sense of identity and pursue their goals (Hwang and Nam 2021). So even if you're not satisfied with their grit level as they head out into the real world, know that it's going to continue to build—if they're doing some of the things covered in this chapter.

Make Them Get Physical

No matter where your teen falls on the grit scale, research suggests that focusing on physical grit first will help develop mental grit, especially in younger kids (Rutberg et al. 2020). This is one of the many reasons why I recommend that all teens participate in sports or a difficult physical activity of some sort. When your teen is pushed to their physical limits at a track meet and they don't think they have an ounce of energy left in them, yet they somehow manage to cross the finish line, they've just built some grit. And their newly found grit is transferrable. They won't only have grit for finishing track races; they now have grit that will help them finish their research paper or work their entire shift at the restaurant. They'll begin to realize that what they learned about their inner reserve of strength by crossing the finish line can be accessed again and again, no matter the situation.

If your teen isn't already in a sport or physical activity, get that going as soon as possible. But remember how important autonomy is! Don't just sign them up for basketball; instead, set guidelines and let them choose within them. Let them know they'll need to do one sport/ physical activity per semester and then let them choose which one. Just make sure you tell them the reasons why (it helps with mood, sleep, and general well-being, plus it'll help them build grit) and that your guidelines are clear. I suggest the following guidelines: whatever they choose must push them by causing an elevation in heart rate and making them sweat, they need to do it a minimum of three days a week including practice and/or games, and there needs to be a coach or trainer involved. These guidelines will ensure that your teen is involved in physical activity that will push them harder than they'd push themselves, which is a key ingredient in grit development.

If your teen is already participating in a sport or physical activity, good work! Support them every way you can. If they want to switch to a different activity, that's fine, as long as the new one meets your guidelines. It's not about turning your teen into the next Simone Biles, it's about helping them push themselves hard physically, no matter what that might look like for your teen. For some, it might mean swimming; for others, bowling or archery. If they're sweating, breathing hard, and have a person providing structure, feedback, and motivation, they're being pushed. If your teen complains that they're not passionate about sports or that they're too busy and stressed to continue playing volleyball, remind them of why it's so important to have a physical activity in their life, or help them with time management so it's less overwhelming.

If your teen is resistant to taking up a sport, there are other ways to build physical grit in your teen. Remember the term *sisu* discussed earlier? It's the Finnish cultural construct that describes a person's ability to push through unbearable challenges (Lahti 2019). *Sisu* and grit both give your teen the capabilities they need to endure adversity, which they'll likely encounter on their way to reaching their goals. Present them with the following list of ways to build *sisu*:

★ **Cold water exposure.** Encourage your teen to use their shower time to build physical grit. Tell them to start off with their preferred temperature and then lower it to as cold as they can tolerate. Have them see how many seconds they can last before going back to their preferred temperature to warm up. Once they're warm, have them see if they can tolerate the cold water for one second longer than the previous attempt, and repeat.

★ **Fasting.** NOTE: Please do not recommend this to your teen if they already struggle with eating issues, tend to restrict food for any reason, or have body image issues that cause them to struggle with eating. If your teen has a healthy relationship with food and doesn't have any physical conditions that would be exacerbated by fasting, they can practice fasting once a month. Have them set a period of time where they'll go without food (water and tea are permitted). Perhaps they will start off with a four-hour block during the day when they don't eat, increase to five hours the next month, six hours the next, etc., until they can handle a twelve-hour fast.

★ **Stimulation removal.** A form of fasting, but instead of avoiding food for a period, they avoid stimulation like screens, spicy foods, and stimulating music. Once a week or once a month, have your teen go on a stimulation-free journey for a set amount of time and gradually build how long it lasts. Instead of watching television, tell them to stare at a blank wall. (Funny, I know, but it's effective!). Instead of adding hot sauce to their dinner, keep it bland. Instead of scrolling on their phones, have them go for a walk without podcasts, music, or conversation.

Consider Environmental Influences

Your teen is heavily influenced by what's in their environment, perhaps even more than you realize. Remember, adolescence is all about independence, social connections, and identity formation. Their brain isn't as future-oriented as you might prefer either. Your teen is likely more concerned about the social dynamics in student government than they are about how many people signed up for the next clean-up day. You might find that your teen puts in more effort to earn driving privileges than they do high grades. But this doesn't have to be a bad thing! Because they're heavily influenced by what's in their environment, you can help them make sure it's full of things that are going to promote overall well-being and grit.

School is probably the biggest environmental influence in your teen's life (outside of parenting). They spend a large amount of time there and receive constant feedback from others. School also provides a lot of the information that your teen consumes. While most of what happens at your teen's school is out of your control, there's plenty of opportunity for your input. Get to know your teen's school by attending parent-teacher conferences, concerts, sporting events, and plays. If possible, volunteer for school events where parents are asked to help. Attending events at your teen's school will give you a window into who they're spending their time with and what the school culture is like. Next, take time to talk with your teen about their school day. Ask questions about what they're learning, what they think of their teachers, and who they're spending time with.

When your teen is learning and setting goals in a mastery-driven school culture where the focus is on progress, not results, your teen gets a chance to develop grit. But if your teen attends a school that focuses on results rather than progress, they're learning that it's okay to stop once they've achieved a desired outcome. For example, if they're in a results-focused environment, they might settle for a C in economics to maintain their current grade point average. They'll do just enough work to get the C, never going above or beyond in assignments or taking time to absorb the material more than the next project requires. Once they've achieved the necessary outcome, they'll stop learning.

But if they're in a school environment that's focused more on mastery than grades, they're learning how to remain focused on a larger aim, rather than stopping once they've achieved a desired outcome. Your teen knows that progress is the expectation, and if they're showing growth, effort, and practice, they're on track. Your teen is challenged to participate in class discussions and to show increased knowledge as they continue through the semester. They're pushed to grasp the material on a deeper level in group projects and essay tests. It's not about grades but about learning and understanding the material. Because the aim is to demonstrate growth, they're developing grit and learning how to stick with a subject that may be difficult or boring. In a mastery-focused environment, they're much more likely to stay committed to learning.

While you likely can't control whether their school culture is progress- or results-oriented, you can control the home culture. If your teen's school is focused on results, help them focus on progress instead. Pay attention to the effort they're putting into their work rather than the grade they receive. Talk about what they're learning in each class instead of what score they got on their last test. Praise effort over outcome and be sure to point out progress when you see it. You can't completely undo the messaging they're receiving at school, but you can challenge it so they think about things a bit differently.

Social interactions are another huge environmental influence and include not just friends but teachers, coaches, teammates, and peers. This is a huge area of influence for your teen because social development is a huge part of adolescent development. If you find that your teen lacks motivation, look at who's in their social sphere. Do they have any friends who appear to be driven or show some grit? Gently encourage your teen to spend more time with those individuals. Does your teen have a teacher or coach they admire? Reach out to those adults and ask for support in increasing motivation in your teen. Are there kids on your teen's team, cast, or band who appear to work harder than others or seem more passionate than most? Point out your observations without judgment or criticism of your own teen and ask your teen how they think the extra work or passion will pay off for the other person. Ask your teen if they feel they have activities or subjects where they put in similar levels of effort or where they feel as passionate. If they don't, get curious as to why and brainstorm ideas on what can be done differently.

When it comes to social influences in your teen's life, how your input will be received depends so much on your delivery and your relationship with your teen. If your teen immediately shuts down whenever you open your mouth, take a step back and see if you can figure out why. Ask your partner, friends, or colleagues about their own observations on how you communicate or what they've noticed when you talk with your teen. Do you tend to do most of the talking? Are your comments and questions full of judgments or criticisms of your teen, yourself, or others? Do you leave room for your teen to respond? Do you allow your teen to fully share their problems or experiences before you jump in with your own thoughts or solutions? These are important questions. If you want to have any influence in the social area of your teen's life, you'll need to ensure that your delivery is compassionate, nonjudgmental, and engaging. And you'll need to create a relationship where your teen values what you offer because they see you living with integrity and doing exactly what you're encouraging them to do.

Finally, we must consider the informational influences in your teen's life. Informational influences include things like social media, television, books, movies, video games, and the internet in general. This content is getting into their brains and their identities. It's shaping their perspective on themselves, others, and the world. And without being overly dramatic here, they're looking at a lot of things you don't know about. I encourage the parents I work with to not only check screen times regularly, but to also look at *where* the time is being spent.

Do this with your teen. How much of their screen time is on social media? How much is spent on games? Pull out your own phone and compare your numbers with your teen's. I also encourage parents to treat their teen's digital life just as they do their teen's real life. Just like you ask questions about what they did at school, ask questions about what they saw online. Did they post or comment on anything on socials? What's going on with the main character in their favorite series? What do they find themselves googling the most lately?

You can model positive informational consumption by watching shows and movies together where the main character overcomes adversity or puts in unfathomable amounts of effort to achieve a high goal. Play podcasts in the car or house that focus on unlocking potential and becoming better versions of ourselves. Share books that you're reading about mindset and see if your teen is interested in discussing this concept further with you. Talk about what they're learning at school and what they think of the topics or subjects. And make sure you're continuing to limit their screen time, so they're not alone in a digital world consuming information that's making them feel awful about their bodies or that they'll never be good enough.

Add Practice and Hope

To help build grit, your teen needs interest, practice, purpose, and hope. When your teen has an interest in the activity or topic, they have a helpful grit intervention already in place. We covered interests (curiosities) at length in the first section, but I want to emphasize the need for your teen to be pursuing something *they* are interested in, not something you're pushing on them. We've also examined the importance of having a purpose and how useful purpose is in helping someone persevere. When your teen has their own *why* behind their actions and feels that they're doing something that's meaningful, they'll put in enduring effort. Now let's look at the two factors we haven't yet covered in this book: practice and hope.

Practice means *deliberate* practice, defined as effortful activity designed to optimize improvement (Ericsson, Krampe, and Tesch-Römer 1993). To achieve deliberate practice, an individual needs a well-defined goal, a level of challenge that exceeds their current ability, immediate feedback, and repeated focus on correcting errors (Hwang and Nam 2021). As you can see, deliberate practice is intentional and requires a bit of planning. This is why I recommend your teen work with a coach or tutor. They need help to create their goals and figure out their level of challenge, which is hard to do solo. Plus, a coach or tutor will provide immediate feedback and opportunities for your teen to make corrections. We can't expect a teen to be able to do these things on their own! And while it might be tempting to step in with your own suggestions, it may not be a good idea in terms of your relationship with your teen. (I know how easily I get annoyed with my husband when he tries to correct my workout routine; however, I'll hear and implement the exact same suggestions from my personal trainer!) The parent's role here is to be supportive.

Hope means your teen believes that their dream or goal can happen and more importantly, that they have a role in making it happen. It's a combination of optimism and growth mindset. Your teen needs to believe in themselves so they can be gritty. Consider what the opposite looks like. Imagine that your teen has a goal of getting a summer job. However, they believe no one would ever hire them because they have no previous work experience and don't have a car to get to and from work. What would this teen do? Would they look and apply for jobs each day? Not if they've decided that there's no point in searching, that there's nothing they can do about it, and they give up before they've even started. Now imagine this same teen has hope. They believe they can get a summer job easily, since they see their peers working. They know they can figure out the public transportation situation if needed, because they've figured out other hard things before. This teen will be applying for summer jobs before the school year is even over. You can instill hope in your teen by pointing out others who are doing or have done the very thing they're pursuing, by talking with them about other hard things your teen has accomplished in life, and by making sure your teen knows you believe in them.

Change a Fixed Mindset

You've learned a lot about fixed versus growth mindsets. Now let's talk about changing mindset; specifically, changing your teen's fixed mindset. In the last chapter, I asked you to notice where a fixed mindset shows up for you. I hope you took some time to do this, because a fixed mindset doesn't just come out of nowhere. If your teen has one in many areas of their life, they developed it at home or school—or both. If they got a bit of it from you, you know where the change needs to start.

You might recall how simply learning about mindset changes our mindset. Talk to your teen about neuroplasticity (the brain's ability to rewire and adapt in response to learning and experience) and how this persists throughout our lifetimes. Talk about how growth mindsets help us catch and rebound from mistakes quicker. And be a living example of a growth mindset at home. When you struggle with a new demand at work, talk about how it's hard right now since you haven't learned the new skills yet, but you know it'll get better with time. If another child in the home is showing strengths in certain areas, praise the effort and practice they're putting in, not the natural talent you think they have or the results they achieve. When you become frustrated with a family member, colleague, or friend who keeps making the same mistake, focus on the skills they haven't yet learned rather than the personality trait you might blame.

When it comes to your teen, catch fixed-mindset self-talk statements. Notice things they say about themselves in their social media posts, while doing homework, or while you're driving them and their friends to the movies. Mindsets can fluctuate—we can have a fixed mindset in one area and a growth mindset in another—so don't assume that a fixed mindset in math means they have it everywhere. But when you hear it pop up, gently (and privately) point it out. Ask them to reframe their thoughts and to think about the situation from a growth perspective instead. If necessary, model what this might sound like. Here are some examples of how you might do this:

★ You overheard your teen discussing trying out for the school talent show with their band and your teen says, "There's no way I could do that! I suck when it comes to performing in front of large groups!"

★ Wait until you have your teen alone and bring it up in a nonconfrontational and nonjudgmental way. You might say, "When I was driving you guys around earlier, I couldn't help but overhear you saying you suck when it comes to performing in front of a lot of people."

★ Pause and wait for them to respond.

★ Work on reframing by saying, "I wonder if there's a different way to think about performing for a big audience. More of a growth mindset way to think about it and less of a fixed mindset." If necessary, remind them of what a growth and fixed mindset are.

★ See what your teen comes up with on their own. If needed, you could offer, "I know it's hard to have a growth mindset all the time. I certainly have to work on it! Maybe for this situation, a growth-mindset perspective might be 'I'm still learning how to perform in front of large groups' or 'Performing in front of a lot of people is a skill I'm still developing.' What do you think?"

★   And then let it go. You don't need to get them to sign up for the talent show or to completely change their mindset right there on the spot. You've planted the seed, but they need to tend to it. When you do this on a consistent basis, you may find they'll start pointing out their own fixed mindset the second you approach them.

Increase Expectations

Increasing expectations is another great way to build grit in your teen. If they don't *have* to do much at home, why would they? Worse, if they know you'll always jump in and rescue them, why bother doing it themselves? And worse still, if you don't expect much of them overall, why would they expect much of themselves? Now, if you're a parent who has chore lists at home that everyone follows, requires that your teen participate in clubs and/or sports each semester, and doesn't allow privileges unless your teen has done all their home- and schoolwork, this section isn't for you. You've put expectations in place and you follow through. Go ahead and jump to the next section. But if you're a parent who doesn't require much participation at home, who doesn't ask that your teen do much at school, or who tends to fix every problem your teen encounters, you'll want to keep reading.

Expectations send messages to your teen. Don't be fooled by their complaining when you set them. Think of that as part of the process. When you set an expectation, you're letting your teen know that you think they're capable of achieving it, even if they don't. You're sending the message that they can handle hard work and are able to figure things out. When you set expectations at home, you're telling them that they're part of the family and you need their help to make it run smoothly. And when you create expectations around schoolwork and activities, they hear those expectations as guidance about what must be good for them, even if they disagree. If you're not used to setting many expectations for them, start with where they're at now and slowly layer on additional things. You don't want to pile on too much at once, which will likely cause so much overwhelm and stress that you'll end up backing off completely, putting you right back where you were when you started.

Here are some guidelines to get you going:

* **Consider your teen's schedule and workload.** What are they lacking? Social activities? Chores? Exercise? Studying? Start with adding in the one area where you'd like to see growth. For example, if your teen isn't getting exercise most days and tends to be inactive, add an expectation around exercise.

* **Make your expectation specific while allowing for autonomy.** For the teen who needs exercise, you wouldn't just tell them they need to get daily exercise. Perhaps tell them they must choose one of the following: a school sport to join, participation in a running program that trains people for a 5K, or going to the gym with you four days a week. You've provided the specifics while giving them the final decision.

* **Follow through.** Once you've set the expectation, check in to ensure it's getting done. If not, why? What are the barriers holding them back? Do they need help signing up for something, a ride, or money? If they're lacking motivation, don't be afraid to throw in a reward. (Remember, adolescent brains are very receptive to incentives!) You may also have to tie certain privileges to their participation.

* **Check in and provide feedback.** Once the expectation has become part of their routine, check in and see how it's going. Ask open-ended questions about their new

responsibility to see how they're feeling and thinking about it. Give positive feedback for effort, no matter how small it may seem to you. Point out any other positive changes you've noticed because of their new effort. Perhaps your teen made new friends through the running program or is managing their time better now.

* **Consider layering on another expectation.** Depending on where your teen started, you might want to add on another responsibility once the first one has become a habit. Go through the same process of considering where they need growth, allowing for autonomy, following through, and providing feedback. You'll know it's time to stop when your teen has less time for the unproductive things like mindless scrolling and video watching than they do for the productive stuff like chores, homework, sports, activities, and friends.

CHAPTER 7

WHAT ARE GOALS?

MOST OF MY CLIENTS LOVE figuring out their passions and discovering their purpose—that's fun! They don't even mind building grit, usually, because they recognize how much they need grit in their life. But they can be less enthusiastic when it comes to setting goals. They will tell me they know what to do or they don't like to plan that far ahead. They'll say goal work is too tedious or a waste of time. And this isn't just my teen clients; I hear the same thing from my adult clients. We covered grit before goals for this very reason: you'll need some grit to get through this section. If you find yourself wanting to jump ship, stay with me. You're going to learn new things about goal setting that will help you transform your teen's motivation.

Goals are the last ingredient of the motivation recipe. Without clear goals, how in the world is your teen supposed to stay on track? If they don't know in which direction to move next, how will they stay motivated to keep going? If they don't know how to break down a huge aim into smaller steps, how will they avoid overwhelm or distractions? Most adults struggle with creating realistic goals; it's much more difficult for teens. Remember, they don't have a fully developed prefrontal cortex, which is the part of the brain responsible for planning, organization, and prioritization—exactly what is needed for setting goals.

Goal setting seems like a pretty simple task. Many people think they can just do it in their heads. I hear teens say all the time, "I know what my goals are! I don't need to write down the steps." What they don't fully understand is how essential it is to write down the steps. First, it reduces the cognitive load of having to remember what to do. They no longer have to remember each step because they offloaded it to a schedule or planner, and now their brain is free to focus on important things like learning, creating, and socializing. Second, they're much more likely to follow through on goals they've written down. Our brains are more likely to encode written information into memory. When your teen puts goals in writing, they become subconsciously aware of what they're working toward, which helps them make decisions that move them closer to their goals (Murphy 2018). Writing down goals, in other words, helps guide and shape our behaviors.

I like to think of my goal sheet as a working document; it will shift and change as my life circumstances change. For example, our beloved rescue bloodhound Watson had to be put down while I was writing this book. We adored this dog more than words can say. I needed to take time to care for him in his final days and then to grieve once he was gone. This meant I had to adapt my goal sheet a bit when I came out of the cloud of sadness. I had specific things that I did not accomplish during the time he was sick, which piled on top of the items I couldn't do while I was grieving. When I was ready, I spent time figuring out what I could let go of, what needed to be moved, and what I needed to do differently to get back on track. I *didn't* say, "Screw it, I'm off track, so why bother?" and throw out my goal sheet. I also didn't sacrifice self-care or life essentials so I could meet my former goals. Goal sheets are meant to be modified when life circumstances take us off track. In chapter 9, we'll cover working with goal sheets and other tools in depth.

Start with the Big Picture

We need to start big so we can go small. Starting big with goals means thinking big picture. It means getting your teen to think about their purpose, and it means helping them figure out what's truly important to them. As was said earlier, it's normal if your teen's purpose is more focused on themselves and less about helping the world. But if we can help them bridge the gap between self and others just a tiny bit, we're helping them create a life purpose.

Since your teen is still forming their identity, you might find that their life purpose shifts and changes. This isn't a sign that your teen is flaky, lacks grit, or is lost. It just means they haven't yet figured out what's important to them. You may find that you're helping them create a new life purpose every few months, and that's totally okay. If that's the case, see if you notice any themes or patterns and help them make the connections.

A life purpose helps your teen in two ways. It increases grit and it gives direction for their goals. When your teen knows their overarching reason for doing the mundane small stuff, they're more likely to put in effort and persevere. If your teen can trace a small daily goal or task all the way back up to their life purpose, they're going to want to do it. And when they know what their life purpose is, they're better able to design their goals. Their life purpose is the overarching idea of what they're trying to achieve, and the smaller goals are all the steps they need to take to get there.

Have a Vision

But we can go even bigger than a life purpose. We can start with a vision. Salim Ismail, Mike Malone, and Yuri van Geest call it the massive transformative purpose (MTP) of successful organizations (2014). A company first identifies what their MTP is (for example, Google's is "to organize the world's information"), which acts as the guiding light for everything else. Google's MTP might sound doable for the company now, but imagine how massive it was at the beginning, when Google was just two people and a laptop. This is the beauty of the MTP: it's visionary. It provides them with a clear statement that guides, inspires, and empowers. It acts as both our fuel and our filter (Diamandis 2023).

Your teen likely has no idea what their MTP is (you might not know yours either!). That's okay. When helping my teen clients create their MTP, I start with helping them figure out what they value (chapter 3), and from there we discuss what's truly important to them in life. (We'll get into how to do this in the action steps in chapter 9.) My professional MTP is "to help people tune out the noise of the world so they can tune into what's truly important to them." Knowing my

MTP, which I have posted on a sticky note on my laptop, inspires me when I work with my clients. It gives me energy to keep going when things are challenging, because I know what I'm striving for with each one. It acts as a filter: when new work requests come in, I can choose the ones that are aligned with my MTP.

Another example of an MTP is Uber's slogan: "The best way to get wherever you're going" (Naude 2017). As you can see, it's not fancy, wordy, or complex. But it's a big idea (massive), shows how the company is going to shake things up (transformative), and gives them direction (purpose).

Your teen's MTP can inspire them toward changing their community or the world for the better. It can give them their *why* and help shape their daily actions. Their MTP is the foundational piece of goal setting. It may sound like something an unmotivated teen has no sense of yet, but in my coaching work, I've found that having a massive vision can help teens set all their goals from huge to small.

Let Your Teen Have Dreams

Huge goals are the catalyst for action. I often hear parents express fears that their teen thinks *too* big. Parents will say to me, "There's no way they're getting into that college, they just don't have the grades. Aren't we just setting them up for failure by encouraging them to set that as a goal?" or "My teen will never make it pro, they just don't put in the practice on the field. Why have them focused on something that they're not even willing to work toward?" My answer is always the same: We *want* them to dream big. We want them to create a few goals that might take years to achieve or may even be impossible. As discussed in chapter 4, we want them to know that we believe they can achieve great things so that they will develop the grit to stick with a passion. To help them with this, we can teach them how to take a huge goal and break it down into smaller and smaller ones, each one becoming more achievable. Meeting these smaller goals will help them achieve great things. Again, grit helps them achieve goals, and achieving goals helps build grit.

Let me give you an example of how this works:

Ty is a middle schooler who barely does his homework. His parents know he could be doing better in school, but can't get him to put in the work. He spends most of his free time playing video games with his friends and complains any time his parents try to get him to do his chores. Desperate to get him motivated for school, they create a new rule where he can't use his devices for non-school activities during the week, and they limit his time on them during the weekends. They also tell him he must choose a school club and sport to join immediately (but leave the choice up to him).

Ty starts attending intramural basketball practices and joins the photography club. After just a few weeks, Ty announces that he wants to play basketball in college. His parents are surprised to learn that his basketball coach is willing to help him create goals around this, since he's barely played and doesn't appear naturally talented for the sport. But with the help of the coach, Ty creates smaller goals tied to his huge goal of playing in college. Together, they consider what needs to happen and create a list that includes playing junior varsity in high school, playing varsity in high school, deciding which colleges he wants to play for, and maintaining a desirable grade point average. Then they break down each of those items. For example, they write down that before Ty can play basketball in high school, he needs to improve his skills. They decide that he needs to pay better attention during the basketball unit of gym class. To pay better attention during the basketball unit, he'll need to work on his focus overall by paying better attention in each of his classes. They agree that he'll need to attend the training programs his middle school offers during the summer and work on his endurance and stamina through cross-training.

They continue breaking down each item until Ty has a clear road map with daily to-do items.

Ty feels energized each day knowing he's working toward his huge goal while being focused on the small steps, since he knows exactly what to do. His parents report that he's more responsible in areas of life outside of basketball as well. They notice he's getting his homework done each day so he has time to practice, doesn't complain about his chores, and gets to bed early most nights. They tell him that if he continues putting in effort, they'll hang up a hoop in their driveway next summer.

Even though playing basketball in college might be an impossible dream, it's easy to see how all the small steps are still helpful for Ty. He's building grit, becoming healthier, improving his focus, and doing something he loves. He's also showing increased responsibility overall. Ty might find that his huge goal changes as he becomes more skilled or spends more time playing basketball. He might find that he'd rather focus on enjoying the sport rather than trying to make a team. He might decide that while he loves basketball, he doesn't want to do it constantly. Or playing basketball may morph into playing baseball, and he exchanges one ball for another. No matter what, he's learning valuable skills along the way—including how to adapt his goals as needed.

Imagine what would have happened if his coach or parents had immediately shot down his college goal? Instead of saying, "Okay, let's consider what needs to be done to get you there," what if the coach had said, "Wow, you've only been playing a few weeks, that's not very realistic"? If the coach had offered a much smaller goal (perhaps simply to "improve your basic skills") instead, that likely would've lacked energy and Ty would have lost enthusiasm and motivation. Or what if his parents pointed out how impossible the college goal was? What if they told Ty that he didn't have the mental focus to do it or that he wasn't at the level of other players his age? His parents would have just handed Ty the perfect excuse to stay unmotivated.

Thinking huge is the fun part of goal setting. Thinking huge gets us in touch with our dreams and lets us imagine a life full of possibility. Your teen gets to see themselves winning the championship, having a best friend, attending their dream school, traveling the world, earning top accolades, or walking through the world with total confidence. Whatever they want for themselves and their future, they get to identify it and put words to it. Your teen, even if they're lacking motivation and direction right now, gets to imagine a future where they shine. They get to articulate what they want for themselves, perhaps for the first time. And then they get to draw the road map that will take them there. Whether or not they reach the destination isn't important right now. All that matters is that they've figured out what lights them up and they have a plan that will help them create the energy they need to move forward.

Huge goals include the things we want to accomplish in the next five years. They might be considered impossible by some. They are related to the MTP in that they'll help us achieve our overall vision. I have huge goals of publishing multiple best-selling books, creating mentorship programs, and getting my digital products into the hands of tens of thousands of people. My huge goals are related to my MTP, but are more specific. However, if you notice, they don't necessarily give me clear direction.

To get clear direction, I take one huge goal at a time and break it down, first into a goal for each year. Take my publishing books goal as an example. I set a goal for the year to finish this book that you're reading now. I might even set another goal of writing another book proposal this year. My yearly goal gives definition to my huge goal and can be traced back to my MTP.

I then take my yearly goals and break them down into quarterly, monthly, and weekly goals, getting more specific with each. My goal sheet ends with a to-do list, which is a list of daily steps that I can check off as I go. I called this breakdown "grunt work" because that's what it feels like while I'm doing it. The MTP and huge goals are the dreamy and visionary stuff; breaking a huge goal down into smaller and smaller goals can feel tiresome and redundant. But this breakdown gives us our road map to follow; when done with care and intention, it makes our journey smooth and easy. Of course, there will be detours and roadblocks along the way, but when we know the destination, it's much easier to correct course. And when we're constantly reviewing, updating, and adapting our route, we find it's easier to travel. I personally love the grunt work aspect of goal setting because I've seen the value in it again and again. I've witnessed countless teens (and adults) reach their huge goals because of their dedication to the process.

Work on Your Own Goals

All this talk about MTPs and huge goals might have gotten you thinking about your own life a bit (or at least I hope it did!). Before we dive into the research and action steps to help your teen in the following chapters, let's do a little work on you first. Because as you know, if you want to help your teen increase their motivation, you need to make sure you're walking the talk first.

DEVELOPING YOUR MTP

This exercise will walk you through the steps I use with my coaching clients to help them develop their MTP. Just remember that this exercise is supposed to be fun and exciting. If it's feeling too much like a struggle or a chore, you or your teen might be approaching it with a negative mindset. Or, perhaps, your teen needs to do it with a different person. Maybe there's an adult in your teen's life, like an aunt, coach, or neighbor, who could guide your teen through this process. You (or the other person) can follow these steps over time and in a way that feels natural. You don't need to sit down at the kitchen table and knock it all out at once. You can flow in and out of these steps in different conversations over several weeks or months.

- **Use the work you did in chapter 3 on developing purpose.** If you haven't yet done it, do the values and purpose exercise with your teen now. This will give you a good foundation from which to build. Don't be afraid to share what you're learning about MTPs and any work you're doing on developing your own. Make this a part of conversations so it doesn't feel like it's coming out of nowhere.

- **Focus on solutions.** Whenever your teen brings up an issue that bothers them, guide them toward solutions. I'm not talking about discounting feelings here or shutting down sharing or venting; those things are important for your relationship. I'm talking about the times when there's an issue that's bigger than them— like other students being treated unfairly, overflowing local animal shelters, or lack of recycling options in your community. Help them brainstorm potential solutions or ask them, "If you had total power in this situation, what would you do?"

- **Share the MTPs of big organizations.** I've mentioned Google's and Uber's already. TED's is "Ideas worth spreading" and Pinterest's is "The world's catalog of ideas." You might search for the MTP or mission statement of their favorite brand. Seeing the grandiosity and simplicity of these statements will give your teen ideas on how to shape their own.

- **Put it all together.** Once they have an idea of what they value, what their purpose is, and the problems of the world that they want to solve, help them put it all together. What's a simple summary of something they want to achieve? They might have several different things, and that's great! Gently share observations of any patterns or themes you've noticed too. For example, when they bring up a lack of recycling options in your community, you might say, "I've noticed how much you care about recycling and I was thinking about how this might fit with one of your core values, leadership. I wonder how these things might go together into a purpose for you?"

- **Help them think big.** Remember what the M in MTP stands for. We want their ideas to be gigantic. Enormous. Bigger than anything they could accomplish on their own. As you're helping them put it all together, encourage monumental ideas and totally audacious solutions. If your teen says, "I want to solve climate change [vision] by finding new ways to recycle [purpose and huge goal]," you've done it right.

CHAPTER 8

A DEEPER DIVE INTO GOALS

TAKE A MOMENT AND REMEMBER a time when your teen had a goal they were working toward. A goal that they chose with a clear desired outcome. It can be a huge goal or a smaller one. Perhaps they wanted to make a sports team or get a spot in the play. Maybe they were trying to earn enough money to purchase something special, or perhaps they were trying to attain a specific grade in a class. When they were focused on reaching that goal, how did your teen behave? What was different compared with times when they weren't focused on a goal? How did they spend their free time when they were working on the goal? What was their general mood like?

Perhaps your teen went to bed earlier during tryouts or auditions. Maybe they spent time planning out their days or weeks as they were earning money. Or perhaps your teen showed less negative self-talk as they worked on attaining their desired grade. Goals give your teen a purpose and help them focus on their future (Emmons 1986). Teens who know what they're striving for think ahead. When your teen has goals, they tend to be more intentional about how they spend their time and feel greater life satisfaction overall (Emmons 2003). They plan things out a bit more and their mood improves. As a parent, you may or not be aware that your teen is doing this, but I can tell you that they most certainly always are. When a teen has clear goals that are aligned with who they want to be, they feel more energized and excited about their days. They notice small bits of progress and feel momentum. They feel focused and proud.

Life Is Better with Goals

We've covered how important it is for a teen to choose their own goals and for the goal to be something they can actually attain (especially if they break it down into smaller steps). The research confirms that adolescents who have goals report greater subjective well-being (Eryilmaz 2011). They experience higher satisfaction with their lives when they're focused on a goal that's important to them (Eryilmaz 2011). But remember, the goal needs to be important to *them*.

I've seen it happen too many times: parents decide their teen needs to achieve certain things, they implement guidelines and rules to make it happen, and they're excited because they know how much this goal will improve their teen's life. The parent tells me about all the positive changes that this goal will create—while the teen sits silently and stares at the floor. The second the parent exits the room, the teen looks me in the eye and says, "Yeah, I'm not gonna work on that." It might be what they need, but if it's not what they want, it's just not going to work. Likewise, it's not whether *you* think it's attainable, it's whether *they* think it is. As we covered in the last chapter, breaking down a huge goal into smaller, attainable steps is going to help a lot with this.

Goals don't just help your adolescent feel better about life; they also give them a sense of pride in their performance, future benefits, and life benefits (Locke and Latham 2002). When a teen expects to reach their goal, they expect other things to come along with it, even if they're not completely aware of these expectations. They expect their goals to improve their life somehow. College students who set a goal of a high grade point average, for example, expect to feel good about their outcomes: they expect to have more career opportunities and career success (Locke and Latham 2002). If your teen sets a goal to have more friends, they might expect that achieving this goal will provide more social opportunities, improve their self-confidence, and help them feel more secure at school. As they're increasing social interactions and expanding their circle, they'll likely also notice that they feel better about going to school and are speaking up more around new people.

Goals Lead to Action

When your teen has goals in place, they have direction. Goals direct your teen's effort and attention toward actions that will help them achieve their goal (Rothkopf and Billington 1979). Not only that, goals help them subconsciously avoid activities that won't bring them closer to their goal (Locke and Latham 2002). For example, many of the teens I coach have goals around creating better habits. We get clear on what better habits look like, which often includes things like putting away screens sixty minutes before bed, getting up with the first alarm in the morning, making healthy food choices throughout the day, and exercising each day. Because they have these clear goals in place, they approach their daily routine with a different perspective. Instead of automatically going out for fast food with their friends for lunch, they'll look for the friend who's staying on campus to eat. Rather than alternating between homework and scrolling until it's time to turn off the lights for the night, they'll finish their homework with time to spare.

Goals also create energy and motivate behavior (Freund, Hennecke, and Mustafić 2019). People who are focused on big goals tend to try harder and take action more frequently. In fact, your teen will put more physical and cognitive effort toward an identified goal, meaning they'll push themselves harder on both levels (Locke and Latham 2002). Your teen won't just feel like they're putting in more effort; physiological indicators will show that they are (Locke and Latham 2002). In other words, subjective and objective data will show that your teen is working hard. Once an unmotivated teen puts a few good goals in place, they may find themselves exerting more physical and mental effort (you'll notice this as well) and doing things that will move the needle in the right direction. Goals increase your teen's energy level and direct that energy toward action.

Teens with goals don't just work harder, they work longer. There's a caveat here: your teen needs some control of the timeline. Research shows that when people have a say in how long they'll work, hard goals help prolong their level of effort (Locke and Latham 2002). If your teen chooses a difficult goal with the full understanding that it will take a long time to achieve, they're more likely to stick with it over time. Likewise, tight deadlines create a more intense and faster work pace (Locke and Latham 2002). Your teen might end up working faster and harder for difficult goals with a short deadline—if that is their choice.

Goals can also increase curiosity in your teen. Trying to accomplish a difficult goal can lead your teen to learning and discovery as they try to figure out each step along the way (Locke and Latham 2002). And since curiosity is one of the components of drive, and so helpful for motivation, we can see how the two play off each other here. For example, perhaps a teen set a goal to get a summer job as a camp counselor and they broke down all the steps they'll need to follow to make it happen. Perhaps some of the steps are easy for them and they do them without any effort, but then they run into a step where they must acquire new knowledge. Let's say they had to learn cardiopulmonary resuscitation. During their training, they learn more about emergency medical work. Then they start to notice whenever an ambulance passes them on the road. They begin asking questions about what paramedics do and what kinds of training and certification they need to go through. By setting a goal of becoming a summer camp counselor, this teen has become curious about a possible career option.

Goals Must Be Adaptable

Goal development looks different depending on which phase of life we're in. Adolescence entails the emergence of an understanding of a future, which is wild to think about. Your teen is just now beginning to imagine their personal future. When your teen was younger, everything felt immediate and short-term; now they are beginning to get a grip on the idea that what they do today could have an impact years later. They still don't have a full grasp on this concept, but their brains are working on it (whether your teen is aware of it or not). You might notice how your own teen sometimes clearly links present behaviors with their future self, yet other times they appear unaware of consequences. Perhaps your high schooler casually mentions that they're trying to improve their study habits so they're better equipped for the increased demands of college. Yet you just watched them eat an entire family-sized bag of chips and then wonder why their stomach ached. But whether they're articulating anything about their future or not, selecting, developing, obtaining, and adjusting goals are a core feature of your teen's life (Gestsdóttir and Lerner 2007).

Self-reported selection refers to how your teen chooses or identifies their goals. To be successful, we want them to select goals they're likely to stick with. Your teen has a broad range of goals that they could choose, so we need to ensure that they're picking ones that align with their passions and purpose. Teens also need to learn how to select an appropriate number of goals. If they have too many, they'll be scattered and overwhelmed. If they have too few, they might be bored or give up when progress plateaus. The right number is going to vary from teen to teen; your teen might need to experiment a bit to find the right amount for them. Once they've selected their goals, they'll need to prioritize them so they know where and how to direct their attention and organize their behavior. They might decide to arrange their goals in order of importance so they're focusing on the most meaningful ones first. Or they might choose to go by a timeline and knock out goals by deadlines instead.

While developing their goals, your teen might experience some friction. Goal conflict happens when your teen is pursuing goals that require different strategies or if their resources are limited (Freund, Hennecke, and Mustafić 2019). For example, let's say your teen is trying to expand their social circle and improve their grades simultaneously. These goals require different skillsets and are competing for a limited amount of free time. As a result, your teen might feel stressed and anxious. Adolescents tend to choose goals that conflict with one another more than adults do, mostly because they haven't learned how to manage their time well yet. When you run into this issue with your teen, help them see the conflict that's occurring and guide them toward prioritizing one over the other.

Once your teen has identified what they're working toward, they'll need to figure out what they must do to obtain their goal. They might focus on logistical resources, like buying a planner to help them better manage their time. Or they might focus on cognitive resources like studying more so they get a higher grade on a test. Adolescents haven't yet built up a huge toolbox, meaning they're likely going to lack a lot of the skills or resources they need to reach their goals. They're going to need support and guidance in figuring out what resources they need and how to acquire them. (We'll cover how to help them with this in the next chapter.)

No matter how excited your teen is about a goal, they're going to get taken off course and need to be able to adjust. They need to be able to adapt and correct course, or they'll never reach any of their goals. Roadblocks and detours are to be expected. When I'm working with a teen client, I build adjustments right into our goal-setting work. I don't wait for roadblocks to happen; I frame them as an expectation. If we think things are going to go perfectly on our quest to achieve, we'll feel disappointed and frustrated and will end up slowing down unnecessarily or even quitting altogether when they don't. However, if we expect that there will be barriers and challenges to overcome, we can plan for them. This way, your teen feels capable and ready to handle the obstacles and is much more likely to keep moving forward.

Goals Must Be Achievable

Whether or not your teen reaches their goals depends on a few things. We have touched on the importance of autonomy: if you want your teen to reach their goals, they need to have control over the goals they're setting. Autonomy gives them the chance to create goals that are aligned with their purpose and to really buy into what they're trying to accomplish. However, if you have specific goals in mind for your teen, you can talk with them about why you think these goals would be beneficial. An assigned goal can be as effective as a chosen one if your teen agrees with the rationale and purpose of the goal (Locke and Latham 2002). If you're assigning a goal, while you are explaining the rationale behind it, make sure you're doing it in a way that's more dialogue and less monologue. Ask your teen for their input. Your teen will hear you better if they feel like you're listening to them as well.

Keep in mind that it's normal for adolescents to focus more on the outcome than the process (Freund, Hennecke, and Mustafić 2019). Later in life, we tend to focus more on the process, but that's not the developmental stage your teen is at just yet. They're going to care about the object or result they're after much more than what happens along the way. This means they're more likely to be motivated by visual reminders of what they're working toward, like pictures hanging on the bedroom wall or images on their lock screen. You also might hear them talking about how life will change once they've achieved their goal. You may find yourself wanting to jump in for a reality check, but I urge you to let them dream. This focus on the outcome is totally normal for their age. If you try to shift focus to all the other things your teen is gaining as they strive toward their goal, they might just hear that their result isn't that important to you.

Your teen also needs a certain level of commitment to reach their goals. In fact, the harder their goal, the more commitment they'll need. Kristen Wiig was seriously committed to her goal of becoming a successful actress, a difficult goal to achieve. If your teen values integrity, making a public declaration about a goal can increase commitment. For example, if your teen declares that they're raising money by running in the school's 5K, they'll be much more likely to follow through even if they've never run before in their life.

Self-efficacy has a big impact on goal achievement too. Mastery is your teen's progress in a particular area, while self-efficacy is your teen's belief in their ability to create progress. The higher the self-efficacy, the higher the self-set goals can be (Phillips and Gully 1997). Your teen needs some skills in place to reach their goal. If your teen doesn't have the necessary skills, they need to believe in their ability to get the skills; otherwise they'll end up frustrated and quit. You can help your teen gain expertise by teaching them, finding classes for them to take, or having them work with a coach or mentor. It also could mean helping them build belief in themselves by providing encouragement or pointing out how far they've come in other areas of life.

Goals need to have a certain level of complexity as well, if we want teens to achieve them. We talked about a challenge/skills balance earlier; that's a good thing to keep in mind here too. It's helpful when goals sit in that sweet spot between being challenging enough that they're not bored, but not so much that they're overwhelmed. We also want teens to have some of the skills needed to reach their goals; however, they don't need to be experts. Remember, a goal sheet is a working document; if your teen sets goals that are too overwhelming or too easy, they can be adapted. If the teen finds they need to acquire a ton of skills first, they can create smaller goals that will lead to the one that they ultimately want to achieve.

You can help them play around with their goals through gentle observations, nonjudgmental suggestions, and helpful guidance. Feedback has been shown to be another crucial element in goal achievement (Locke and Latham 2002). People need information on how they're progressing (or not). If we're logging how many books we read each month, we can easily see if we're on track to meet our goal. This feedback creates momentum and we keep moving forward. But if we're not, we now can reflect on why and see what changes we need to make. Feedback allows us to identify barriers, figure out where we're getting stuck, and adapt as needed. Feedback might also come in less direct forms. Perhaps your teen is working on building new friendships and their feedback comes from how much eye contact they're making or whether they spoke to anyone new that day. Whether their feedback is trackable data points or subtle social cues, it provides valuable information for achieving goals.

Now that you have a solid understanding of the benefits of goal setting, as well as the framework for goal achievement, it's time to move forward into action steps.

CHAPTER 9

HELPING YOUR TEEN ACHIEVE GOALS

IN THIS CHAPTER, I COVER action steps that research shows are helpful for most teens (and adults too!), but it's not always a one-size-fits-all situation. You might have discovered unique action steps that only work for your teen; just because they're not included here doesn't mean they're not good to use. You can use the information in this chapter to build off what you know already works, add to your repertoire, or be your total guide. Just as with everything else, mindset matters! If you approach this information with the mindset that it is going to help positively change things for your teen, you'll both get much more out of it.

Creating the Right Goals

The MTP isn't a goal, it's a vision. Next, we're going to break the vision down into goals. We're going to start with distant goals (huge goals) that your teen wants to achieve in the next five years and break those all the way down to goals your teen can achieve in a week. When it comes to huge, yearly, and quarterly goals, we're not going to worry too much about how doable they are. But for the monthly and weekly goals, we'll want to make sure we're helping your teen create ones that are achievable.

There are a few things to keep in mind with monthly and weekly goals. First, your teen needs to be aware of the level of difficulty of each. Remember the challenge/skills balance, that sweet spot where your teen is challenged enough but not overwhelmed. We want their goals to challenge them, but we don't want them to feel impossible, which can cause your teen to lose all motivation and give up. Their larger goals (quarterly, yearly, huge) might feel overwhelming or impossible at this point, but we're not focusing on those right now.

We also want to ensure self-efficacy with your teen's goals. Your teen needs to believe in their ability to achieve their goals. As you're mapping it out and creating smaller and smaller achievable goals, if your teen starts to realize how capable they are of reaching their monthly or weekly goals, you're on the right path. Your teen needs to believe that they either have the necessary skills to reach their goal or that they know how to acquire those skills. Perhaps they have a goal this year of making the school's dean's list. When you help them break this down, it includes a monthly goal of getting all missing assignments turned in. This may seem difficult to them. But as you talk through how they'll work toward this goal and set some weekly goals, they may think of ways to accomplish those goals. Perhaps they'll realize there's a tutor who can help with the homework for the harder classes or that they can use their free time a couple of days after school to focus on completing older assignments.

The challenge/skills balance goes along with self-efficacy, as does mindset. If your teen is lacking the necessary skills to achieve a goal, they're likely going to lack belief in their ability to carry out the needed actions. If your teen tends to view themselves more negatively or thinks they're not capable of learning, they'll see most goals as too hard. You'll need to assess where your own teen is at with both their challenge/ skills balance and their mindset and help them create goals that they see as doable. Remember, it's not whether *you* see it as doable; your teen needs to believe they can achieve it. This might mean breaking goals down further and further into smaller and smaller steps. Once your teen expresses an attitude of "Okay, I got this," they've achieved goal self-efficacy.

Finally, we need to consider what resources your teen needs to reach their goals. Since they've already thought about what skills are necessary, they may know what resources they need. Maybe your teen has a goal of making the football team next fall and sets a monthly goal of practicing at the local field house every day after school. Do they need a membership? A ride? Help them see what they need and have them brainstorm possible solutions. You're not jumping in and figuring everything out for them; you're pointing out things they haven't yet considered. Maybe you know they don't have a lot of free time right now. Rather than come out and say that, ask them to pull out their schedule and see where they'll fit in practices at the field house. You're also not being the negative voice telling them why their goals aren't doable; you're asking how they plan to get the things they'll need. Perhaps they need a membership, but you know you don't have the budget for that right now. How else can they get in football practice? Is there a gym at their school they can use instead? Do they know someone on the team who could work with them once a week? Helping them figure out what resources they'll need is a proactive way of keeping them on track.

GOAL BREAKDOWN PRACTICE

As always, it helps if parents are also doing this work. So before we go on, grab some paper and a pen and do this exercise.

- Write down your MTP that you identified in chapter 7. If you haven't done that yet, take a moment and consider what yours might be. What problem do you hope to solve during your lifetime? What do you want your legacy to be? What acts as your guiding light? You can create 1-3 different MTPs. No need for perfection here.

- Choose one of your MTPs and consider—what are some huge goals you're working toward that are directly related to it? What are things you want to accomplish in the next five years? Just jot down some ideas here.

- Choose one of your huge goals and break it down into goals you can accomplish in the next year.

- Break your yearly goals down into what you can accomplish in the next quarter.

- Break your quarterly goals down into what you can accomplish in the next month.

- Break your monthly goals down into what you can accomplish next week.

- Create action items out of your weekly goals. This will be your to-do list.

Road Mapping

Once you have an understanding of what goals should look like for you, you're ready to break things down. Think of the MTP as the top of the summit; now it's time to figure out the route to get there. Be forewarned: The road to the top might be long and winding. It might have lots of stops and twists and turns. It might be difficult to navigate. If this is the case for your teen, that just means you're doing it right. Your teen's summit is so high and so important, it requires off-road detours and stops. If your teen is trying to solve climate change, for example, they're going to have an extremely long road and need a pretty big map. There are going to be lots of offshoots and different directions to explore. And this map will need to be adjusted as they go. They might bump into dead ends or barriers that are so big, they must do a complete reroute, rather than just take a detour.

Creating a road map with your teen should be a fun process. It's exciting to think of all they're going to accomplish! But since it can be a bit tedious at times, break it up and work on it in chunks over time, rather than doing the entire thing in one sitting. It can be helpful if you have an example to use first instead of just diving straight into your teen's road map. This could be an example from your own life, or you could map out the route of a character from a show or movie together. Either way, we want the example to be one that provides a nice frame-work for your teen, so they get an idea of what they're trying to achieve. Perhaps you might use Jessica Watson (the teen who sailed around the world solo and unassisted) as your guide. You could first watch the movie or read the book about her story together (both are titled *True Spirit*) and, once you're ready to work on road mapping, talk about what her MTP likely was (to inspire others by sailing around the world solo and unassisted). You write that on the top of a sheet of paper. You then brainstorm together all the things she had to accomplish to make that happen and, using figure 1, discuss where on the road map each thing would fit. You don't have to get it absolutely correct. This is just to give your teen an idea of how the framework looks and works. (Note: For simplicity, there's only one box for each level of goals shown in figure 1. You can of course add as many as you need.)

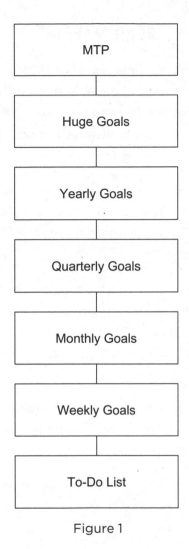

Figure 1

Once your teen understands the framework, you're ready to dive into creating their road map. Take it slow. Some parents work on this with their teens over Sunday morning brunch at their favorite restaurant or when they go out for coffee together as a special treat. Some work on this just a few minutes at a time after dinner or while waiting in the car for a sibling to finish soccer practice. You can get creative with when and how to do this! If you approach it as a helpful tool that will get your teen where they want to go, they'll be willing to do it.

ROAD MAPPING

- Call the first road map a draft so your teen is willing to make mistakes and play around with it. When we label something a draft, we automatically understand it as a work in progress, which decreases the pressure to get it right.

- Put their MTP at the top and talk about what they'd need to accomplish in the next five years to make it a reality. Those things go in the Huge Goals box under each MTP.

- Think about what needs to happen in the next year to achieve each huge goal. List those out in the Yearly Goals box. (For some huge goals, they might have lots of yearly goals. For others, they might have very few.)

- Now, what needs to happen in the next three months to achieve each yearly goal? Those things go into the Quarterly Goals box.

- What needs to happen in the next month to achieve each quarterly goal? Those go into the Monthly Goals box.

- Breaking it down even more, what needs to happen in the next week for each monthly goal? Write these items in the Weekly Goals box.

- Having done that, what needs to get done tomorrow? Those items go into the To-Do List box.

- Congratulations! Now, if necessary, repeat the process for each MTP on a different sheet.

You can see why this process needs to be broken up over time and made fun. Otherwise, your teen is never going to want to go through this process. It's time-consuming and often tedious. But it also helps your teen with time management, planning, and organization. It gives them a chance to see all the steps they need to follow, how maps will adapt and change over time, and how their daily actions are connected to their overarching MTP. Once they have each Huge Goal mapped out all the way to the To-Do List, talk to them about scheduling their daily items into their calendars so they learn how to plan and manage their time better. Encourage them to cross items off as they complete them. Talk to them about using their goal sheet each day to help prioritize what needs to be done the next day.

Finally, make the road map a regular part of your check-in with your teen. Discuss what they've accomplished from the different goal boxes and what needs to be adapted. Perhaps they could put up a road map for the one huge goal they're focused on currently on a whiteboard in their room. Maybe you help them create a spreadsheet for all the other huge goals. Maybe you make a weekly coffee date where you both pull out your road maps and plan out your week accordingly. No matter how you go about it, just make sure that road map check-ins are a part of your weekly or monthly routine with your teen. Otherwise, it'll get pushed aside and your teen will forget about it.

Staying on Course

Goal setting is a tedious and laborious process. Just creating a goal sheet takes grit! But the beauty is, once we have our goal sheet, we have our map. We know what our plan is, and we have steps to follow each day. It keeps us on track. I like to take fifteen minutes at the end of each day to consider my to-do list items for the next day. I cross off what I achieved that day, move things to the next day's schedule if needed, and create my list for tomorrow. This new list gets scheduled into my calendar, so I know if I'm being realistic about the time I have available. And boom! I now have my map for the next day in place. I just need to wake up and look at my schedule. It literally tells me exactly what I need to do that day. So I'm constantly working toward my huge goals and MTP. The nightly review is on my schedule to do at the end of each day so I don't forget.

Another strategy to staying on track is doing a monthly review. At the end of each month, I take about thirty minutes to consider the previous month. I look at the big picture first and consider how I spent my time, where I struggled, and where I achieved big things. I then focus in on the details and identify which goals I worked toward, which ones I haven't even thought about, and the barriers that got in my way. I pull out my goal sheet and see where I need to make changes. If I've met any goals, I cross them off. I schedule this monthly review at the end of each month on my calendar. You can use a journal or a spreadsheet for this monthly review.

Use Scheduling Tools

Planners, calendars, and schedules are essential elements to staying on track. These tools reduce our cognitive load. Most of us can't keep a lot of tiny detailed information in our short-term memory, which is the part of memory immediately available to us. There's a limit to the amount of information we can process at any given time; if we have too heavy of a cognitive load, we don't learn or recall information effectively. This is even more true for teens, whose brains aren't yet fully developed. Trying to rely on memory is not only a waste of resources, but also inefficient. We'll always forget, lose, or miss something. Relying on a tool, like a planner, to reduce cognitive load frees our brains up to do the things they're good at: creating, analyzing, and interpreting.

Remember, it's going to be hard to motivate your teen to do something that you refuse to do yourself. What's your system for staying on track? Do you have a whiteboard hanging up in the kitchen where you track everyone's activities, appointments, and events? Do you have a calendar, whether paper or electronic, that you're constantly pulling out to check? Or do you feel overwhelmed as you try to manage your day without a system in place? This is a good time to consider what's working and what's not when it comes to your schedule. Because without a good schedule in place, you won't be able to stay on track with your goals either.

If you don't already have a planner, get one as soon as possible! I personally love the ones with a monthly overview and then the weekly view that breaks down each day into hours. I use the monthly view to keep track of bills and trips; the weekly view is where I plan out each day. And when I say plan out each day, I mean my *entire* day is accounted for—showering, driving, client sessions, writing, hiking, checking emails, breaks—it's all on there. Blocking out the time for each task helps me know what I have time for, what's truly possible. To be honest though, I only do this type of scheduled planning on workdays. When it's not a workday, I schedule in writing time, CrossFit classes, and any specific errands or appointments I may have, but I leave a lot of open spaces on the calendar. (Yes, this sounds like a lot of work up front, but once you get the hang of it and have a system in place, it's easy to maintain.)

I always encourage my clients to use paper planners, since research shows we remember more when we write things down by hand. Plus, I think it's easier to look ahead in a physical planner. We're also less likely to get distracted by other things when we're using a paper planner; when people use a digital calendar, they often end up checking emails, looking at news, or getting lost in notifications. They forget why they even opened their laptop or phone to begin with! But if you absolutely cannot convince your teen to go old-school, digital is fine. Whether they use digital or paper, make sure the planner shows times for the entire day. We don't want them using planners that have just a giant blank box for each day.

Once they've settled on what they're going to use for their planner, you might find that you need to teach them how to use it. I've found that many teens don't know how to use a planner. They'll write important due dates in, but not much else. Start by sitting down with your teen and walking them through how to write in appointments, practices, clubs, games, etc. Teach them how to write things at the correct time rather than just listing everything on one day. Show them how to block out the total amount of time they'll need for each item. For example, if they have a dentist appointment scheduled for Tuesday at 4 p.m., talk about how long it'll take to get there and back home and then block out that entire amount of time. Have them write in the due dates for anything coming up, both big and small. See if there are any other important things coming up that they want to include, like birthdays, anniversaries, or social gatherings.

Next, show them how they can take just a few minutes each day to plan out their next day. Have them look at their weekly goals and their to-do lists. Where can each item fit into their schedule? Again, make sure they're not just listing things out. We want them blocking time. If they plan to complete a college essay, for example, how much time do they think they'll need? If they need two hours, which two hours will they use? Block that out. Have them also plan out the specifics of their study time. Instead of just blocking out 6 p.m. to 8 p.m. for schoolwork, write in exactly what they'll do during that time (for example, "chem lab report, read two chapters, study for math test"). By getting specific with what they'll do during that time, they're learning how long things take. They will get more and more accurate with practice.

Do Regular Check-Ins

Your teen is going to need some help to maintain the plan. In the beginning, you'll likely have to remind your teen each night to pull out their calendar to plan the next day. You'll have to sit down with them on the weekend to figure out their next week's plan. But the more you do it and make planning sessions a regular occurrence in your house, the quicker it turns into a habit.

If you don't have a relationship with your teen that allows for a weekly or monthly check-in without fighting, you may want to bring in some outside help. Hire a coach, enlist the school counselor, or ask a relative who has a good relationship with your teen to step in and help. Your teen is learning major life skills when they work with you or someone else on goal-setting. They're learning how to plan, prioritize, organize, and manage their time. Plus, as we learned in the last chapter, goal-setting is good for their psychological well-being.

Besides planning their time, your teen will need to learn how to plan for roadblocks and detours. Barriers are a normal part of the goal process. We don't want to count on things going smoothly, otherwise your teen will be completely thrown off course when they don't. Instead, we want to anticipate what might go wrong and have a plan in place. This way your teen won't be surprised when a problem pops up and will know exactly what to do. This applies only to the logistical details of goal-setting, not the visionary aspects. For example, when my athlete clients have a huge goal of making it to a certain level—like getting a spot on the Olympic team—we don't plan for what to do if they don't make it. Instead, we look at the smaller details and plan accordingly. If their monthly goals include a certain number of training hours outdoors, what will they do if the weather is awful? How will they still be able to train? Or if they're planning to work with a specific teammate or train with a partner, what will they do if that person can't make it?

Look at your teen's goal sheet with them and consider some of the logistical aspects. Ask them to identify potential barriers that might prevent them from meeting their weekly or monthly goals. Is it a time issue? How might schoolwork get in their way? What about when they just feel exhausted? Once they've identified some roadblocks, talk with them about how to handle each one. They don't need to write anything down, and this can be done over dinner, car rides, or while walking the dog. Just getting them to think about what they can do when they encounter these roadblocks gives your teen the cognitive resources they will need to handle them. This isn't about telling them things won't work, but rather teaching them how to identify probable roadblocks so they know how to go around them. See what your teen comes up with first and then offer some of your own ideas.

CHAPTER 10

PUTTING IT ALL TOGETHER

MOTIVATION CONSISTS OF THREE SEPARATE skillsets: drive, grit, and goals. Drive includes your teen's curiosities, passions, purpose, autonomy, and mastery. Grit is your teen's ability to persevere over the long haul and stick with their interests consistently. And goals are your teen's road map that can help them figure out how to connect their vision and purpose to their daily life. Your teen might be lacking in one, two, or all three of the skillsets. This book gives you the tools to not only figure out where they are weak, but to help them get stronger in those areas too.

If you find that your teen isn't interested, willing, or able to do some of the work I've suggested, please don't lose hope or think your teen is doomed. Instead, I want you to know that this won't always be the case for your teen. Start with where your teen is at currently, do things in bits and chunks, and know that big things are still possible for them.

Here are some suggestions for what you can do right now:

* If your teen isn't **curious** about much, give them space, time, and exposure to lots of different activities and topics. Maybe they need stricter screen limits so they have more time to explore things in real life. Or perhaps they're so overscheduled with things *you* want them to do that there's not enough time for them to find what *they* want to do. Help them create time on their schedule and then step back and let them explore.

* To help your teen cultivate **passions**, point out when you notice them engaging in something they truly seem to enjoy. Ask open-ended questions to get them thinking about those things. Help them figure out which aspects of it they love and where those aspects show up in other activities. If their passions are healthy, encourage them to spend more time in them. If your teen is completely

lacking passion, create a list of possible interests and have them spend twenty minutes a day on a chosen item from their list for two weeks, tracking their own thoughts and feelings along the way in a journal.

★   If your teen needs help with their **purpose**, do the values audit from chapter 3 to help them figure out what their core values are. Point out whenever you notice passions lining up with their core values and help them make connections between their values and something bigger. Remember that it's normal if your teen's purpose is more focused on self; however, you can help them see how their purpose might benefit others or the greater good.

★   When your teen needs more **autonomy**, you likely need to take a step back. Make sure your expectations and guidelines are clear, but then allow your teen to work within them, however that might look for them. Allow your teen to screw up and make mistakes. Give them the opportunity to fix things on their own, without you jumping in to rescue or doing all the work for them. Have family meetings where everyone's voice is heard and create more autonomy-supporting environments for your teen.

★   To help your teen with **mastery**, point out all the hard things they've done before and help them figure out their process. Talk about how that process might fit with other hard things they're working on. Teach your teen about the challenge/skills balance and ask open-ended questions about where they fall on the spectrum of overwhelm to boredom with certain activities. Encourage them to create balance within their daily or weekly schedule so it's not too heavy on one end or the other.

★ When your teen lacks **grit**, get them engaged in some form of daily physical activity immediately. Keep *sisu* in mind and have them do things like cold-water exposure or stimulation removal. Remember the impact of environmental influences and consider whether those influences are positively or negatively impacting their ability to stick with things. Hire a coach to ensure your teen is getting deliberate practice in while you instill hope through your belief that they can do hard things. And don't be afraid to increase expectations at home.

★ If your teen needs **goals**, buy a good paper planner and then start with the massive vision. Help them map out their own course from the MTP all the way down to their daily to-do list. The distant goals (huge, yearly) can be outside the realm of possibility for now, but we want the monthly and weekly goals to feel doable. Your teen needs to believe in their ability to achieve goals; if necessary, keep breaking them down until they feel doable to your teen. Talk about potential roadblocks and create plans for getting around them. Make road map check-ins a fun weekly activity and help them make any needed changes.

★ Remember that **mindset** is essential. From developing curiosities, passions, and purpose to building mastery and becoming grittier, your teen needs to learn how impactful their thoughts and attitude are. Make the word *neuroplasticity* a part of your family's vocabulary and talk about how everyone is always growing and changing through learning and experiences. Monitor your own self-talk and point out when either of you is approaching things with a fixed mindset.

A Final Word About Environment

This book has covered quite a bit about environmental influences on your teen and how much things like friends, teachers, coaches, social media, and general news consumption impact their personality. Hopefully, you've been examining the influences in your teen's life and how those things might be impacting their perspective and attitude, and helping them adjust as needed. But I want you to also consider their physical environment. Research shows that our psychological health is negatively affected by clutter, artificial lighting, crowding, and noise in our environments (Saxbe and Repetti 2010).

Think about your teen's bedroom or the space where they tend to do their work. Is it organized, or is there lots of clutter? Do they have much exposure to natural light, or is it mostly overhead lighting? Is there are a lot of stuff crammed into a small area, or is there room to move around? Are they exposed to constant noise from others, or do they have the option to keep it quiet?

An ideal space would have minimal clutter, be clean, have natural lighting (or have lamps versus overhead or fluorescent lighting), have ways to keep things organized, and be free from distracting sounds. If you're realizing just how bad their space is, talk to your teen about how having a clean and organized space will help increase their motivation and make life easier. And then plan a day (or week) where you'll help them get things in order. Start with the area that will most help with motivation first, like their desk, and then move to other spaces, conquering one at a time.

As you're helping your teen clean up their space, consider other areas of the house as well. How do *you* feel when you walk through the door? If you find that you're easily distracted by the objects in your home, you'll have a hard time following through on things. If you feel overwhelmed with clutter or house projects, you won't be motivated to do much. And if you're feeling overwhelmed and unmotivated, imagine how your teen must be feeling. We want our homes to be as restorative as possible. We don't want them to be sources of overwhelm.

Here are some tips to help clean up your home, which you can do with your teen. By having them help with these chores, they'll gain a sense of being involved in the running of the home and will also learn how to do it in their own space, now and in the future.

★ Recycle or donate items that no one's used for the last six months. If you haven't worn or used it, let someone else get some use out of it.

★ Limit the number of sentimental items on display. You don't need to display *every* family photo or put out every ornamental gift someone has given you. If you can't part with it, put it in storage or have a box for the decorations you rotate by season.

★ Keep surfaces clean from dust and clutter. Research shows that we think better when our space is clean. Make dusting and decluttering a regular part of the weekly routine. (To increase autonomy, have everyone sign up for a different chore each week, or have a chore wheel that gets rotated weekly.)

★ Create a "landing" and "loading" zone. This might be a basket by the back door where your teen drops their bookbag when they get home and can put their sports gear for the next day. Or it could mean a bowl on the counter for keys and wallets so no one has to spend time hunting for things at the last minute. No matter what you use, keep it in the same location.

★ If possible, have separate spaces for work and relaxation. Beds should be for sleeping, desks for working. If your teen is using their bed for both work and sleep, their brain might get confused. Is it trying to focus for work or is it trying to shut down to sleep? Prevent your teen from working in their relaxation space by setting up another area for work, like a desk or at the kitchen table. Or maybe have them go to the local library or stay after school if your house tends to be busy or full of distractions.

★ Set expectations for how they keep their own bedroom while honoring their autonomy. It's not about controlling the content of their room (like what types of posters or pictures they hang up), but rather helping them stay on top of clutter and disorganization. Expectations might include keeping dirty clothes in a hamper, putting away clean clothes within forty-eight hours of washing them, removing dirty/used dishes every night and putting them into the dishwasher, and being responsible for weekly vacuuming and dusting of their space.

A Final Word to You, the Parent

I know you're walking a fine line here. You want your teen to learn things on their own, but you don't want them to miss out. You want them to make progress, but you don't want to do everything for them. You want to push them hard enough to move forward, but not too hard that you damage your relationship. Parenting is hard and parenting teens is even harder. I hope that the information in this book has been helpful for you and gives you the tools you need to not only help your teen, but to also feel better about yourself as a parent. Because I know you're a good one. I know because I work with parents like you every day and I hear their fears of messing up, ruining their teen's life, or failing as a parent. I will tell you what I tell them: You're not failing.

You're not. You're doing the absolute best you can with the information you have *and* you're learning and growing along the way. Cut yourself some slack.

As you implement some of the things you've learned in this book, you'll likely run into lots of moments where you'll want or need to provide your teen with feedback. It may be feedback on how to improve a specific skill or it could be in the form of observations. No matter what you're providing feedback on, *how* you approach it will determine how your teen receives it. If you and your teen tend to argue a lot and don't communicate well, they'll be more likely to be put off by your feedback. We want your teen to see your feedback as valuable information that will help them grow. Realistically, that's not always going to be the case, no matter how perfectly you approach it or how great your relationship is.

So it's important to first do a "vibe check" on your teen's mood and attitude. They're going to be much more receptive to your input if they're in a decent mood and generally feeling good about life. If they've had a bad day or are feeling down on themselves, any feedback you provide is likely to be perceived negatively, even if it's constructive and useful. Wait until they've come out of their bad mood a bit before diving in and offering your thoughts. It can also be helpful to ask if they're open to it. Try asking, "Do you want my feedback on the situation/what you're doing?" This gives them a choice whether to listen or not. If they say yes, they're mentally prepared to hear what you have to say. You're not catching them off guard. And when they're ready for your feedback, frame it as your own observations, not the absolute truth; you might say, "It seems to me…," or perhaps "It looks like…"

If your relationship with your teen is a little rocky and they perceive many of your comments negatively, you'll need to work on that before you offer much feedback. They're going to immediately tune you out if they assume you think they do most things incorrectly. Work on improving communication with your teen by doing small things together with minimal pressure, like running errands or making dinner, while discussing random topics where neither of you has a strong opinion. Staying focused on safe topics gives you both the chance to learn how to listen better, since no one's getting heated or worked up. It also opens the door to getting to know each other more since you'll get to hear one another's insights and thoughts. You can also use the stories and characters from movies, shows, books, or celebrity events to offer indirect feedback. This is safer since it's not directly about your teen. Just make sure it's actual feedback (observations on how to improve a skill or area of life), rather than judgmental opinions (harsh, critical statements).

As you're helping your teen increase their motivation, remember that this journey is going to require times when you'll need to step back and let go. You'll set the expectations, but then you'll need to let them figure out how to work within those expectations. You'll offer input and guidance, but then you'll need to let go as they decide whether to listen. Just as plants require sunlight and water to grow, teens require space and independence.

If a parent is constantly hovering over their teen, micromanaging their schedule and activities, giving them an exact script on what to say to a friend or teacher, or ensuring that all their free time is filled with activities or screens, that parent may be doing a true disservice to the teen and their future. An overly solicitous parent may be robbing the teen of opportunities to learn and grow by taking away the very experiences that they need the most, preventing them from figuring things out, and even worse, instilling the belief in themselves that they're not capable of doing hard things.

I know this isn't your intention. I know that's not what you want to do. There's a lot of societal pressure to micromanage kids, and you may see other parents doing just that. But you don't have to be like other parents. You get to decide how you want to parent your teen. Ask yourself what kind of adult you want your teen to become. If the answer includes them being motivated, resilient, and knowing how to deal with adversity, then you know what to do. If you find that you need some extra support in the details, I'm just an email away. You can always reach out to me at connect@destinationyou.net or through my website, https://www.destinationyou.net.

I'm rooting for you. And I can't wait to see the positive impact your teen has on the world.

REFERENCES

American Psychological Association (APA). n.d. "APA Dictionary of Psychology." https://dictionary.apa.org.

Baard, P. P., E. L. Deci, and R. M. Ryan. 2004. "Intrinsic Need Satisfaction: A Motivational Basis of Performance and Well-Being in Two Work Settings." *Journal of Applied Social Psychology* 34(10): 2045–2068.

Blackwell, L. S., K. H. Trzesniewski, and C. S. Dweck. 2007. "Implicit Theories of Intelligence Predict Achievement Across an Adolescent Transition: A Longitudinal Study and an Intervention." *Child Development* 78(1): 246–263.

Burgess, K. 2010. "Sailor Abby Sunderland, 16, Crosses the Equator; Jessica Watson, Also 16, Nears Southern Point of Africa." *Los Angeles Times*, February 22. http://latimesblogs.latimes.com/outposts/2010/02/abby-sunderland-1.html.

Burrow, A. L., R. Sumner, and M. Netter. 2014. "Purpose in Adolescence." *ACT for Youth Center of Excellence*. https://www.actforyouth.net/resources/rf/rf_purpose_1014.pdf.

Casey, B., S. Duhoux, and M. M. Cohen. 2010. "Adolescence: What Do Transmission, Transition, and Translation Have to Do with It?" *Neuron* 67: 749–760.

Cauffman, E., E. P. Shulman, L. Steinberg, E. Claus, M. T. Banich, S. Graham, and J. Woolard. 2010. "Age Differences in Affective Decision Making as Indexed by Performance on the Iowa Gambling Task." *Developmental Psychology* 46(1): 193–207.

Chen, P., Y. Lin, D. J. H. Pereira, P. A. O'Keefe, and J. F. Yates. 2021. "Fanning the Flames of Passion: A Develop Mindset Predicts Strategy-Use Intentions to Cultivate Passion." *Frontiers in Psychology* 12: 634903.

Coatsworth, J. D., and D. E. Conroy. 2009. "The Effects of Autonomy-Supportive Coaching, Needs Satisfaction, and Self-Perceptions on Initiative and Identity in Youth Swimmers." *Developmental Psychology* 45(2): 320–328.

Csíkszentmihályi, M. 1975. *Beyond Boredom and Anxiety.* San Francisco: Jossey-Bass.

Damon, W. 2008. *The Path to Purpose: How Young People Find Their Calling in Life.* New York: Simon & Schuster.

Deci, E. L., and R. M. Ryan. 1985. *Intrinsic Motivation and Self-Determination in Human Behavior.* New York: Springer.

Dewar, G. 2023. "The Authoritative Parenting Style: An Evidence-Based Guide." *Parenting Science.* https://parentingscience.com /authoritative-parenting-style.

Diamandis, P. H. 2023. "Build a Massive Transformative Purpose: A Purpose Statement for Yourself & the World." https://www .diamandis.com/mtp.

Duckworth, A. L. 2013. "Grit: The Power of Passion and Perseverance." TED Talks, April. https://www.ted.com/talks /angela_lee_duckworth_grit_the_power_of_passion_and _perseverance.

———. 2016. *Grit: The Power of Passion and Perseverance.* New York: Simon & Schuster.

Duckworth, A. L., C. Peterson, M. D. Matthews, and D. R. Kelly. 2007. "Grit: Perseverance and Passion for Long-Term Goals." *Journal of Personality and Social Psychology* 92(6): 1087–1101.

Duckworth, A. L., and D. S. Yeager. 2015. "Measurement Matters: Assessing Personal Qualities Other Than Cognitive Ability for Educational Purposes." *Educational Researcher* 44: 237–251.

Dweck, C. S. 1986. "Motivational Processes Affecting Learning." *American Psychologist* 41(10): 1040–1048.

———. 1999. *Self-Theories: Their Role in Motivation, Personality, and Development*. New York: Psychology Press.

Elkind, D., and R. Bowen. 1979. "Imaginary Audience Behavior in Children and Adolescents." *Developmental Psychology* 15(1): 38–44.

Emmons, R. A. 1986. "Personal Strivings: An Approach to Personality and Subjective Well-Being." *Journal of Personality and Social Psychology* 51(5): 1058–1068.

———. 2003. *The Psychology of Ultimate Concerns: Motivation and Spirituality in Personality*. New York: Guilford.

Ericsson, K. A., R. T. Krampe, and C. Tesch-Römer. 1993. "The Role of Deliberate Practice in the Acquisition of Expert Performance." *Psychological Review* 100(3): 363–406.

Erikson, E. H. 1968. *Identity: Youth and Crisis*. New York: Norton.

Eryilmaz, A. 2011. "Investigating Adolescents' Subjective Well-Being with Respect to Using Subjective Well-Being Increasing Strategies and Determining Life Goals." *Journal of Psychiatry and Neurological Sciences* 24: 44–51.

Freund, A. M., M. Hennecke, and M. Mustafić. 2019. "On Gains and Losses, Means and Ends: Goal Orientation and Goal Focus Across Adulthood." In *The Oxford Handbook of Human Motivation*, 2nd ed., edited by R. M. Ryan, 280–300. Oxford: Oxford University Press.

Gardner, M., and L. Steinberg. 2005. "Peer Influence on Risk Taking, Risk Preference, and Risky Decision Making in Adolescence and Adulthood: An Experimental Study." *Developmental Psychology* 41(4): 625–635.

Gestsdóttir, S., and R. M. Lerner. 2007. "Intentional Self-Regulation and Positive Youth Development in Early Adolescence: Findings from the 4-H Study of Positive Youth Development." *Developmental Psychology* 43(2): 508–521.

Glaveski, S. 2019. "Stop Letting Push Notifications Ruin Your Productivity." *Harvard Business Review*, March 18. https://hbr.org/2019/03/stop-letting-push-notifications-ruin-your-productivity.

Good Life Project. n.d. "How to Develop Resilience and Grit." https:// www.goodlifeproject.com/articles/resilience-and-grit.

Grolnick, W. 2003. *The Psychology of Parental Control: How Well-Meant Parenting Backfires*. New York: Psychology Press.

Gruber, M., and Y. Fandakova. 2021. "Curiosity in Childhood and Adolescence—What Can We Learn from the Brain." *Current Opinion in Behavioral Sciences* 39: 178–184.

Hektner, J. M., and M. Csíkszentmihályi. 1996. "A Longitudinal Exploration of Flow and Intrinsic Motivation in Adolescents." Paper presented at the Annual Meeting of the American Educational Research Association, New York, April.

Hill, P. L., A. L. Burrow, and K. C. Bronk. 2016. "Persevering with Positivity and Purpose: An Examination of Purpose, Commitment, and Positive Affect as Predictors of Grit." *Journal of Happiness Studies* 17: 257–269.

Hoeschler, P., U. Backes-Gellner, and S. Balestra. 2018. "The Development of Non-Cognitive Skills in Adolescence." *Economics Letters* 163: 40–45.

Hwang, M., and J. K. Nam. 2021. "Enhancing Grit: Possibility and Intervention Studies." In *Multidisciplinary Perspectives on Grit*, edited by L. E. van Zyl, C. Olckers, and L. van der Vaart. New York: Springer.

Ismail, S., M. S. Malone, and Y. van Geest. 2014. *Exponential Organizations: Why New Organizations Are Ten Times Better, Faster, and Cheaper than Yours (And What to Do about It)*. New York: Diversion Books.

Kern, M. L., L. Benson, E. A. Steinberg, and L. Steinberg. 2016. "The EPOCH Measure of Adolescent Well-Being." *Psychological Assessment* 28(5): 586–597.

Kotler, S. 2021. *The Art of Impossible: A Peak Performance Primer.* New York: Harper Wave.

Lahti, E. 2019. "Embodied Fortitude: An Introduction to the Finnish Construct of Sisu." *International Journal of Wellbeing* 9(1): 61–82.

Locke, E. A., and G. P. Latham. 2002. "Building a Practically Useful Theory of Goal Setting and Task Motivation: A 35-Year Odyssey." *American Psychologist* 57(9): 705–717.

Loewenstein, G. 1994. "The Psychology of Curiosity: A Review and Reinterpretation." *Psychological Bulletin* 116(1): 75–98.

Murphy, M. 2018. "Neuroscience Explains Why You Need to Write Down Your Goals if You Actually Want to Achieve Them." *Forbes*, April 15. https://www.forbes.com/sites/markmurphy /2018/04/15/neuroscience-explains-why-you-need-to-write -down-your-goals-if-you-actually-want-to-achieve-them.

Naude, D. 2017. "A List of Massive Transformative Purposes." *Medium*, October 2. https://medium.com/dawidnaude/a-list-of -massive-transformative-purposes-or-purposii-purpii-16859dff64c5.

O'Keefe, P. A., C. S. Dweck, and M. W. Walton. 2018. "Implicit Theories of Interest: Finding Your Passion or Developing It?" *Psychological Science* 29(10): 1653–1664.

Padham, M., and I. Aujla. 2014. "The Relationship Between Passion and the Psychological Well-Being of Professional Dancers." *Journal of Dance Medicine and Science* 18(1): 37–44.

Pantzar, K. 2022. *Everyday Sisu: Tapping into Finnish Fortitude for a Happier, More Resilient Life.* New York: TarcherPerigee.

Phillips, J. M., and S. M. Gully. 1997. "Role of Goal Orientation, Ability, Need for Achievement, and Locus of Control in the Self-Efficacy and Goal-Setting Process." *Journal of Applied Psychology* 82(5): 792–802.

Pink, D. H. 2009. *Drive: The Surprising Truth About What Motivates Us.* Prestonpans, GB: Canongate Books.

Rothkopf, E., and M. Billington. 1979. "Goal-Guided Learning from Text: Inferring a Descriptive Processing Model from Inspection Times and Eye Movements." *Journal of Educational Psychology* 71: 310–327.

Rutberg, S., L. Nyberg, D. Castelli, and A. K. Lindqvist. 2020. "Grit as Perseverance in Physical Activity Participation." *International Journal of Environmental Research and Public Health* 17(3): 807.

Ryan, R. M., and E. L. Deci. 2000. "Self-Determination Theory and the Facilitation of Intrinsic Motivation, Social Development, and Well-Being." *American Psychologist* 55(1): 68–78.

Saxbe, D. E., and R. Repetti. 2010. "No Place Like Home: Home Tours Correlate with Daily Patterns of Mood and Cortisol." *Personality and Social Psychology Bulletin* 36(1): 71–81.

Seligman, M. E. P. 2011. *Flourish: A New Understanding of Happiness and Wellbeing.* London: Nicholas Brealey Publishing.

Steinberg, L., E. Cauffman, J. Woolard, S. Graham, and M. Banich. 2009. "Are Adolescents Less Mature Than Adults? Minors' Access to Abortion, the Juvenile Death Penalty, and the Alleged APA 'Flip-Flop.'" *American Psychologist* 64: 583–594.

Stern, H. 2021. "Interview with Kristin Wiig." *The Howard Stern Show* (radio show), February 10.

Stone, D. N., E. L. Deci, and R. M. Ryan. 2008. "Beyond Talk: Creating Autonomous Motivation Through Self-Determination Theory." *Journal of General Management* 34(3): 75–91.

Tang, X., M. Wang, J. Guo, and K. Salmela-Aro. 2019. "Building Grit: The Longitudinal Pathways Between Mindset, Commitment, Grit, and Academic Outcomes." *Journal of Youth and Adolescence* 48: 850–863.

Tirri, K., and T. Kujala. 2016. "Students' Mindsets for Learning and Their Neural Underpinnings." *Psychology* 7(9): 1231–1239.

Twenge, J. M. 2017. *iGen: Why Today's Super-Connected Kids Are Growing Up Less Rebellious, More Tolerant, Less Happy—and Completely Unprepared for Adulthood—and What That Means for the Rest of Us.* New York: Atria Books.

Von Culin, K. R., E. Tsukayama, and A. L. Duckworth. 2014. "Unpacking Grit: Motivational Correlates of Perseverance and Passion for Long-Term Goals." *Journal of Positive Psychology* 9(4): 306–312.

Vukasović, T., and D. Bratko. 2015. "Heritability of Personality: A Meta-Analysis of Behavior Genetic Studies." *Psychological Bulletin* 141(4): 769–785.

Melanie McNally, PsyD, is a licensed clinical psychologist and brain coach who helps adolescents build self-awareness and create authentic goals for a fulfilling future. She is a strong advocate for teen mental health, and has been a panelist at the White House, speaking about youth mental health needs. She is founder of Destination You, where adolescents and their parents can access support through virtual coaching and books. She is author of *The Emotionally Intelligent Teen.* She also speaks to audiences of all sizes about how to increase emotional intelligence and motivation in teens.

Real change *is* possible

For more than forty-five years, New Harbinger has published proven-effective self-help books and pioneering workbooks to help readers of all ages and backgrounds improve mental health and well-being, and achieve lasting personal growth. In addition, our spirituality books offer profound guidance for deepening awareness and cultivating healing, self-discovery, and fulfillment.

Founded by psychologist Matthew McKay and Patrick Fanning, New Harbinger is proud to be an independent, employee-owned company. Our books reflect our core values of integrity, innovation, commitment, sustainability, compassion, and trust. Written by leaders in the field and recommended by therapists worldwide, New Harbinger books are practical, accessible, and provide real tools for real change.

MORE BOOKS from
NEW HARBINGER PUBLICATIONS

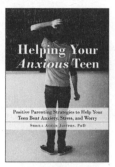

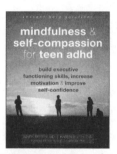